YORK NOTES

THE MERCHANT OF VENICE

WILLIAM SHAKESPEARE

NOTES BY MARTIN J. WALKER

 Longman

 York Press

The right of Martin J. Walker to be identified as Author of this Work
has been asserted by him in accordance with the
Copyright, Designs and Patents Act 1988

YORK PRESS
322 Old Brompton Road, London SW5 9JH

PEARSON EDUCATION LIMITED
Edinburgh Gate, Harlow,
Essex CM20 2JE, United Kingdom
Associated companies, branches and representatives throughout the world

© Librairie du Liban *Publishers* 1997, 2002

First published 1997
This new and fully revised edition first published 2002
Fourth impression 2004

10 9 8 7 6 5 4

ISBN 0-582-50616-6

Designed by Michelle Cannatella
Illustrated by Clyde Pearson
Map by Martin Ursell
Chart by Kathy Baxendale
Typeset by Land & Unwin (Data Sciences), Bugbrooke, Northamptonshire
Produced by Pearson Education Asia Limited, Hong Kong

CONTENTS

PREFACE

York Notes are designed to give you a broader perspective on works of literature studied at GCSE and equivalent levels. With examination requirements changing in the twenty-first century, we have made a number of significant changes to this new series. We continue to help students to reach their own interpretations of the text but York Notes now have important extra-value new features.

You will discover that York Notes are genuinely interactive. The new **Checkpoint** features make sure that you can test your knowledge and broaden your understanding. You will also be directed to excellent websites, books and films where you can follow up ideas for yourself.

The **Resources** section has been updated and an entirely new section has been devoted to how to improve your grade. Careful reading and application of the principles laid out in the Resources section guarantee improved performance.

The **Detailed summaries** include an easy-to-follow skeleton structure of the story-line, while the section on **Language and style** has been extended to offer an in-depth discussion of the writer's techniques.

The Contents page shows the structure of this study guide. However, there is no need to read from the beginning to the end as you would with a novel, play or poem. Use the Notes in the way that suits you. Our aim is to help you with your understanding of the work, not to dictate how you should learn.

Our authors are practising English teachers and examiners who have used their experience to offer a whole range of **Examiner's secrets** – useful hints to encourage exam success.

The General Editor of this series is John Polley, Senior GCSE Examiner and former Head of English at Harrow Way Community School, Andover.

The author of these Notes is Martin J. Walker, an English Teacher, examiner and journalist. He has worked on the GCSE English and English Literature examinations since the start of GCSE in 1988 and is now a senior examiner.

The text used in these Notes is the Longman Literature Shakespeare edition, edited by Laura Hutchings (Longman, 1992).

PART ONE

INTRODUCTION

HOW TO STUDY A PLAY

Though it may seem obvious, remember that a play is written to be performed before an audience. Ideally, you should see the play live on stage. A film or video recording is next best, though neither can capture the enjoyment of being in a theatre and realising that your reactions are part of the performance.

There are six aspects of a play:

1. THE PLOT: a play is a story whose events are carefully organised by the playwright in order to show how a situation can be worked out

2. THE CHARACTERS: these are the people who have to face this situation. Since they are human they can be good or bad, clever or stupid, likeable or detestable, etc. They may change too!

3. THE THEMES: these are the underlying messages of the play, e.g. jealousy can cause the worst of crimes; ambition can bring the mightiest low

4. THE SETTING: this concerns the time and place that the author has chosen for the play

5. THE LANGUAGE: the writer uses a certain style of expression to convey the characters and ideas

6. STAGING AND PERFORMANCE: the type of stage, the lighting, the sound effects, the costumes, the acting styles and delivery must all be decided

Work out the choices the dramatist has made in the first four areas, and consider how a director might balance these choices to create a live performance.

The purpose of these York Notes is to help you understand what the play is about and to enable you to make your own interpretation. Do not expect the study of a play to be neat and easy: plays are chosen for examination purposes, not written for them!

EXAMINER'S SECRET
Remember that a play was written to be performed, not simply to be read. The characters are open to interpretation.

AUTHOR – LIFE AND WORKS

1564 William Shakespeare is baptised on 26 April in Stratford-on-Avon, Warwickshire

1582 Marries Anne Hathaway

1583 Birth of daughter, Susanna

1585 Birth of twins, Hamnet and Judith

1590–3 Early published works and poems written when theatres are closed by Plague

1594 Joins Lord Chamberlain's Men (from 1603 named the King's Men) as actor and playwright

1595–9 Writes the history plays and comedies

1597 Shakespeare buys New Place, the second biggest house in Stratford

1598 Writes *The Merchant of Venice*

1599 Moves to newly-opened Globe Theatre, writes *Twelfth Night*

1599–1608 Writes his greatest plays, including *Macbeth*, *King Lear* and *Hamlet*

1608–13 Takes over the lease of Blackfriars Theatre and writes final plays, the romances, ending with *The Tempest*

1609 Shakespeare's sonnets published

1613 Globe Theatre burns down 29 June, during performance of *Henry VIII*

1616 Shakespeare dies, 23 April, and is buried in Stratford

1623 First Folio of Shakespeare's plays published

CONTEXT

1558 Elizabeth I becomes Queen of England

1568 Mary Queen of Scots is imprisoned for life

1577–80 Sir Francis Drake becomes the first to circumnavigate the world

1587 Mary Queen of Scots is executed

1588 Defeat of the Spanish Armada

1591 Tea is first drunk in England

1593–4 Outbreak of the Plague in London, closing theatres and killing as many as 5,000 people, according to some sources

1594 Queen Elizabeth spends Christmas at Greenwich and is entertained by the leading theatre company of her day, headed by James Burbage, William Kempe and Shakespeare

1595 Walter Raleigh sails to Guiana

1599 Oliver Cromwell is born

1603 Elizabeth I dies on 24 March; James I, son of Mary, succeeds to throne of England

1604 Peace treaty signed with Spain

1605 The Gunpowder Plot

1611 The Bible is translated into the Authorised (King James) Version

1614 Fire sweeps through Stratford but New Place is spared

1618 Thirty Years War begins

SETTING AND BACKGROUND

Shakespeare was a very successful and famous man in his own day. He was a favourite playwright of Queen Elizabeth and of her successor, James I. His careful cultivation of royal approval and his links with the Earl of Southampton gave him a privileged position. Shakespeare's plays were well liked by the public and he became very wealthy. It is difficult to think of a modern equivalent of Shakespeare, but famous film-makers such as Steven Spielberg and Orson Welles are probably our closest equivalents. By today's standards, Shakespeare was a self-made millionnaire, a difficult achievement in the twentieth century and a remarkable one for the sixteenth.

WHY VENICE?

In Shakespeare's time, Venice was the most important trading centre in the world. Goods from the Far East were traded in Venice and with them came new ideas and discoveries. The great explorer Marco Polo was Venetian and he had opened up trade routes with many new countries. To the English, living on an island and frequently cut off by war, the land we know as Italy held a great fascination. Italy was seen as a fashion centre and, largely because of its Roman history, as a centre of culture. Remember that at this time in England, only the wealthy had baths, and then perhaps only once a year, and that it was considered normal to be stitched into your clothes for the winter. Compared to England, Italy was a stylish and rather mysterious place.

THE JEW IN ENGLAND

The explanation of Shakespeare's portrayal of Shylock is not a simple one. Today we think of different religions existing side by side as normal and desirable. This was not the case in Shakespeare's day. For one thing there were not really any Jews living in England at this time. They had all been taxed to the point of poverty and finally banished, three hundred years before Shakespeare.

The idea of a Jew as used in *The Merchant of Venice* is not based upon observations of real Jews. By the time the play was written, only the old, medieval idea of a Jew existed for people in England. The word

 CHECK THE NET
Log on to the Shakespeare Birthplace Trust (**www.shakespeare.org.uk**) and see Shakespeare's baptism and marriage entries and his signature.

 DID YOU KNOW?
The Merchant of Venice was written and first performed in the England of the late sixteenth century, yet it remains one of the most frequently performed plays today.

EXAMINER'S SECRET

You will gain more credit if you show you have some understanding of the play in its historial context.

DID YOU KNOW?

Italian comedies in the sixteenth century were full of life and wit.

'Jew' had come to be applied to hard-hearted, unscrupulous moneylenders, even though the people referred to were not Jewish.

VENICE AND BELMONT

Venice is a city, whereas Belmont is Portia's house, set some distance away. This idea is consistent with the fact that wealthy people had a home in London, which they used when they had business at Court, and a country estate. Women would often have remained in the country when their husbands went to London and this helps to account for the idea that Belmont is very much run by a woman.

SHAKESPEARE'S USE OF SOURCES

Most of the plot elements of *The Merchant of Venice* appear in stories translated from French and Italian. As there are great similarities between Shakespeare's story and some of these accounts, it seems highly likely that Shakespeare had read, or at least heard of them. 'Il Pecorone', which literally translated means 'blockhead', tells of a wealthy young man named Gianetto visiting the port of Belmont, in a ship supplied by his friend Ansaldo. There he meets a beautiful, rich widow about whom he hears that any man who can 'possess' her will win her wealth and her hand.

To finance his attempt to win the Widow of Belmont, Gianetto is obliged to borrow money from his friend Ansaldo. As Ansaldo's money is all invested in ventures abroad, he is forced, in turn, to borrow money from a Jewish moneylender. The story of the pound of flesh appears here exactly as it does in *The Merchant of Venice*.

It also includes an account of the lady dressing as a lawyer and outwitting the Jewish moneylender and the business with the rings which occurs in Act V of *The Merchant of Venice*.

An Elizabethan audience would have been quite happy at the misfortunes of a Jew, a Spaniard and a Moor. Shakespeare was clearly giving the public what it wanted.

Now take a break!

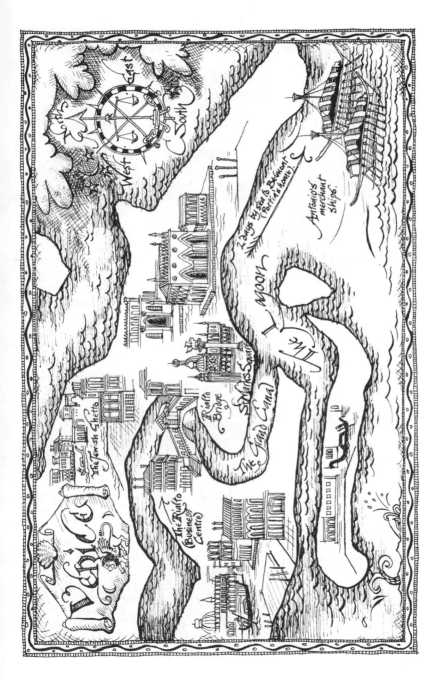

Act I

1 Antonio and Bassanio discuss Portia

2 Portia and Nerissa discuss suitors

3 Shylock and Antonio, the bond

Key to symbols used in table

Scene set in Venice

Scene set in Belmont

Antonio and Shylock; the pound of flesh

Portia and the caskets; who will win Portia's hand?

Lorenzo and Jessica; betrayal and elopement

Portia and Bassanio, Nerissa and Gratiano; the rings used as a test of loyalty

Act II

1 Portia meets Morocco

2 Lancelot joins Bassanio

3 Jessica prepares to run away

4 Lorenzo hears Shylock is away

5 Shylock leaves for the feast

6 Lorenzo and Jessica elope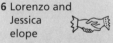

7 Morocco chooses a casket

8 One of Antonio's ships is lost at sea

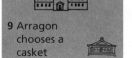

9 Arragon chooses a casket

Act III

1 Shylock hears of Antonio's losses

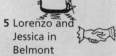

2 Bassanio, caskets and Antonio

3 The arrest of Antonio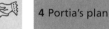

4 Portia's plan

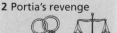

5 Lorenzo and Jessica in Belmont

Act IV

1 The trial

2 Portia's revenge

3 A test for the lovers

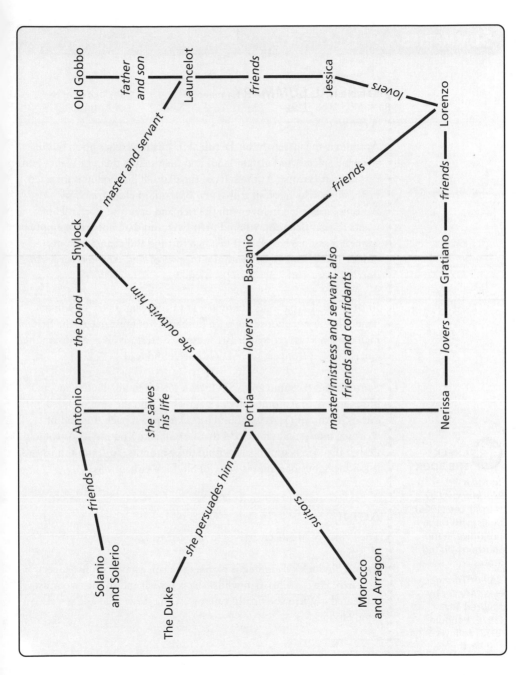

PART TWO

SUMMARIES

GENERAL SUMMARY

ACT I

Antonio is the merchant of the title. His business relies upon buying silks and spices from distant lands and then selling them in Venice and throughout Europe. At the start of the play, all his money is invested in his ships, which are all still at sea. Bassanio, a close friend of Antonio, has fallen in love with the rich and beautiful Portia. He wants to visit Belmont, where Portia lives, but dare not arrive empty-handed. Bassanio has wasted his own fortune and a large sum of money loaned to him by Antonio. In spite of this, Antonio agrees to borrow money and give it to his friend.

In Belmont, Portia waits nervously as various suitors try to win her hand. She cannot choose her own husband, but must marry the first man to pass a test set by her late father. The test involves choosing the correct casket from caskets of gold, silver and lead.

Antonio and Bassanio go to Shylock, a Jewish moneylender and a bitter enemy of Antonio. Shylock agrees to lend the sum of 3,000 ducats if Antonio is to be bound by law to pay it back. Instead of charging interest, Shylock says that he will take a pound of Antonio's flesh if the loan is not repaid within three months. Antonio thinks this is kindness, but Bassanio is wary of Shylock's intentions.

ACT II

The Prince of Morocco arrives to take the test.

Jessica, Shylock's daughter, is planning to run away with her lover Lorenzo. He is a Christian whilst she is Jewish and so the two must act secretly. When she finally runs away, she steals gold and jewels from Shylock.

CHECK THE BOOK

To Kill a Mockingbird by Harper Lee (1966) deals with racial prejudice in the southern United States.

Roll of Thunder, Hear My Cry by Mildred Taylor (1976, Penguin 1977) follows a similar theme.

Morocco chooses the gold casket – the wrong choice. Bassanio sets sail for Belmont as a second suitor, the Prince of Arragon arrives there. Arragon chooses the silver casket and also fails the test.

ACT III

The news that one of Antonio's ships has been lost at sea delights Shylock, who begins to think that he might now have his revenge upon Antonio for the terrible way in which the merchant has treated him over the years.

Bassanio arrives in Belmont and, for the first time, we see a suitor whom Portia would like to marry. She desperately wants him to choose the correct casket, but cannot give him any help. Bassanio selects the lead one and in it finds a portrait of Portia, showing he has chosen wisely. Bassanio's companion has, meanwhile, fallen in love with, proposed to and been accepted by Nerissa, Portia's maid. Before the couples can celebrate their marriages, a letter arrives from Venice saying that all Antonio's ships have been lost and that Shylock is intent upon having his bond. The men leave for Venice to try to pay Antonio's debt. They are wearing rings given to them by their wives.

Shylock has Antonio arrested and taken to court. Portia sends to her cousin, Doctor Bellario, for the costume of a lawyer and a letter ·recommending her to the Duke of Venice. She and Nerissa travel to Venice to help Antonio. Lorenzo and Jessica remain in Belmont with Launcelot.

ACT IV

In court, no one is able to make Shylock change his mind about the bond. Not even the Duke of Venice can persuade him. Portia and Nerissa arrive, disguised as a lawyer and his clerk. Portia plays along with Shylock, saying that he is entitled to take a pound of Antonio's flesh. She cleverly makes him insist on following the absolute letter of the law. Effectively Shylock is tricked into behaving without mercy. He is also fooled into incriminating himself regarding his desire to kill Antonio.

CHECK THE NET

Explore the main sights of Venice and discover its history at **www.venetia.it**

EXAMINER'S SECRET

When writing about a specific scene or extract always make connections with the play as a whole – this at least shows you have read the complete work!

As Shylock is about to take his knife to Antonio, Portia says that he must not spill so much as one drop of blood as blood is not mentioned in the bond. Shylock has been caught out by his own insistence that the bond be upheld absolutely.

Shylock has lost and is punished for attempted murder by the confiscation of his wealth and by being forced to convert to Christianity. He does not appear again.

ACT V

Portia and Nerissa insist upon being given the rings that Bassanio and Gratiano are wearing, as payment for saving their friend.

Portia and Nerissa arrive back in Belmont just before their husbands and pretend that they have never been away. The wives ask to see that their husbands are still wearing the rings they were given. Of course, Portia and Nerissa actually have the rings. Bassanio and Gratiano are humiliated in front of Antonio, who has accompanied them, but all ends well when the wives admit to their joke.

Now take a break!

DETAILED SUMMARIES

SCENE 1 – Bassanio has a problem

1 Antonio is troubled and his friends try to raise his spirits.

2 Bassanio explains his problems regarding Portia.

3 Antonio agrees to borrow money in order to help his friend.

We are introduced to Antonio's business. The idea of disaster at sea leaving a merchant penniless hints at future events.

In Venice, three friends Antonio, Salerio and Solanio are discussing their nervous feelings about one of Antonio's merchant ventures. Salerio and Solanio are ambitious and want Antonio to notice them.

Antonio says 'In sooth, I know not why I am so sad' (line 1). Lorenzo, Gratiano and Bassanio arrive and his friends joke with him. Lorenzo senses that Antonio and Bassanio wish to be alone, though Gratiano fails to take the hint. Lorenzo finally persuades Gratiano to leave with him.

> **CHECKPOINT 1**
>
> Why is the possibility of losing everything because of misfortune at sea clearly shown here?

 **DID YOU KNOW?**

In some editions Salerio is Salarino.

> **GLOSSARY**
> **sooth** truth

? **DID YOU
KNOW?**
Classical references
such as this and the
comparison of
Portia to the wife of
Brutus (Caesar's
friend, assassin and
'the noblest Roman
of them all') would
have been
understood by
educated members
of Shakespeare's
audience and
establish that
Bassanio is himself
an educated man.

Antonio and Bassanio now discuss the matter which has been
troubling Antonio. Antonio asks his friend to tell him of the lady to
whom he has sworn 'a secret pilgrimage' (line 120). They talk about
the rich and beautiful Portia. Bassanio mentions that Portia is rich
before he says that she is beautiful. He seems as interested in her
wealth, as in her. Several of the references he uses to describe her are
related to wealth, e.g. the Golden Fleece of the Jason and the
Argonauts story.

Bassanio faces a problem in attempting to woo Portia. She has
attracted the interest of many wealthy men and if Bassanio does not
act quickly he could lose out. As her other suitors are rich, Bassanio
feels that he cannot arrive at Belmont without money. Not only has
Bassanio squandered his own fortune, he has borrowed money from
Antonio which he is unable to repay. Bassanio argues that if Antonio
were prepared to loan him yet more money, he could use it to make
his fortune and repay both debts to Antonio. Bassanio illustrates this,
lines 139–51, with the idea of shooting an arrow in the same direction
as one that has been lost, 'and by adventuring both, I oft found both'
(lines 143–4).

Antonio is quite prepared to lend his friend the necessary money but
all of his fortune is invested at sea, and he does not have such funds
readily to hand. He suggests that they try to find out whether such
money is available in Venice and borrow it in his name.

SCENE 2 – Portia and her suitors

1 Portia lists her suitors and makes fun of them.

2 The will is explained.

3 Portia hears of the arrival of the Prince of Morocco.

In Belmont, Portia begins by complaining about her situation. She is
quickly reminded by her servant and friend, Nerissa, that she is
actually very fortunate and should concentrate on keeping a level
head. Portia says that it is easy to give advice but much more difficult

to follow it. Portia's father has stated in his will that Portia cannot choose her own husband, but instead she must marry whichever man chooses the correct of three caskets.

Nerissa then asks her mistress if she has affection for any of her suitors. Portia launches into a savagely witty attack upon the men who have presented themselves so far:

- The Neapolitan Prince talks only of his horse.

- The County Palatine does nothing but frown.

- The French Lord does everything to excess. Portia says that he would drive her mad.

- Falconbridge, a young English baron, does not speak any of the languages that Portia speaks. He is good looking, but dressed in a mixture of styles from different countries.

- The Scottish lord has done nothing but fight with the Englishman.

- The German, the Duke of Saxony's nephew, is described as a drunkard.

Portia dreads having to marry any one of these suitors.

Fortunately, these men did not like the terms of Portia's father's will and have recently left Belmont. Here, Nerissa reminds Portia of a young Venetian soldier who had visited Belmont in her father's time. Portia remembers his name instantly 'Yes, yes, it was Bassanio, as I think so was he called' (line 111), though she tries to play down her interest in him. Portia is ready to say more about Bassanio, but is prevented from doing so by the news that the Prince of Morocco is on his way. Portia says of him, 'I had rather he should shrive me than wive me' (lines 124–5).

Portia is a very witty character as is shown by her remarks about her suitors.

In today's terms Portia appears to be racist, attacking several national characteristics. In Elizabethan England, this would have been a perfectly acceptable way of creating humour.

CHECKPOINT 2

Why is Nerissa Portia's **confidante** as well as her servant?

GLOSSARY

shrive me than wive me hear my confession rather than marry me

The only man Portia has ever shown any interest in is Bessanio, hinting at later plot developments.

> ### Ideas about marriage
>
> Portia is not able to choose her own husband. This was quite usual for ladies at this time.
>
> Arranged marriages were normal for wealthy people. Marriage was often carried out like a business transaction.
>
> Portia's latest suitor is black with 'the complexion of a devil' (line 124). The Elizabethans found dark skin repulsive and a common insult was to say that someone was sunburnt. People applied white lead to their faces to be fashionable; many died of lead poisoning.
>
> It would have been unthinkable for a highly placed lady such as Portia to have married a black man.

SCENE 3 – The meeting with Shylock: the bond

❶ **Antonio and Bassanio visit Shylock so that Antonio can borrow money.**

❷ **Shylock lends the money but asks for a very strange bond.**

> **CHECKPOINT 3**
>
> Bassanio and Shylock speak in **prose**, but change to the more formal verse when Antonio enters. Why?

This is the first entrance of Shylock to whom Bassanio has gone to borrow money. Shylock is interested to hear that Antonio will be responsible for repaying the debt. He manages to hide his hatred for the Christians, though he does warn that 'I will not eat with you, drink with you, nor pray with you' (lines 34–5). Shylock is well informed about Antonio's business, and is fully aware that all the merchant's money is invested at sea. The Jew reflects upon the disasters which might befall a ship at sea and then decides to take Antonio's bond.

Shylock says of Antonio, 'I hate him for he is a Christian' (line 38) and plans to take revenge upon him for the ill-treatment that he has

received from the Christians. Shylock is often picked on because he lends money and charges interest; something the Christians are not allowed to do.

Antonio does not like doing business with the Jews. He is also very much against moneylending. He is forced to borrow money from Shylock and this angers him, especially when Shylock reminds him that Antonio has said that he would neither lend nor borrow money at interest.

Shylock justifies his business by telling a story from the Bible. Jacob was asked to look after his uncle Laban's sheep. He was told that he could keep any lambs which were born streaked or pied in colour. When the sheep were mating, he made a fence which was striped. The sheep saw this as they conceived and so the lambs were born with striped coats. Jacob was able to keep many more lambs than he might otherwise have done.

Antonio warns Bassanio that 'The devil can cite Scripture for his purpose' (line 94). Antonio is quickly reminded by Shylock that he requires a favour from the Jew. Shylock then exploits the situation and recounts at length the ill treatment that he has received at the hands of Antonio. Antonio has:

DID YOU KNOW?

The 'devil' reference is both a common insult and an anti–Semitic one.

GLOSSARY

complexion of a devil Morocco is black and Elizabethans believed that devils were black

cite Scripture recite the Bible

Scene 3 continued

- Often insulted Shylock in public because of the Jew's occupation
- Called him 'misbeliever' because of his Jewish faith
- Spat upon Shylock's coat
- Spat in Shylock's face
- Kicked him as though he were a dog

EXAMINER'S SECRET

Remember it is easier to learn in small doses than commit everything to memory at once.

Shylock asks whether a dog would be able to lend Antonio the money that he needs, and whether Antonio now expects him to be humble like a slave and give him the money.

Instead of remaining calm through this, Antonio loses his temper. Christians could attack Jews openly, whereas the laws of Venice prohibited Jews from retaliating. Perhaps this is one reason why Shylock is better at controlling his temper than is Antonio. The merchant asks Shylock to lend the money 'not / As to thy friends' (lines 128–9) but as if he were lending it to an enemy.

Shylock offers Antonio a deal which appears to come out of friendship. He says that he will forgive and forget the insults and the attacks made upon him. The deal is this:

- Antonio and Shylock are to go to a lawyer and sign a 'bond' (line 141).
- Antonio will be legally bound by the bond.
- The bond is in 'merry sport' (line 141) only.
- If Antonio cannot repay the bond by the due date, he will forfeit a pound of flesh.

Bassanio is wary of Shylock's sudden kindness, but Antonio agrees to the Jew's terms without hesitation. Shylock says that he would have nothing to gain if the bond were forfeit as a pound of human flesh is worthless. Antonio is unconcerned about forfeiting the bond as his ships are due home 'a month before the day' (line 177).

Antonio's ability to repay the loan is dependent upon his ships returning home safely.

The conversations in Scene 1 about possible disasters at sea now become much more significant.

The balance of power shifts between Antonio and Shylock in this scene. Shylock manages to achieve the upper hand.

> ## Moneylending
>
> Christians were forbidden from lending out money in order to profit from it. Today people borrow money from banks and expect to be charged interest on the amounts borrowed.
>
> Jews were tolerated in society because their religion allowed them to act like modern banks. This caused much resentment among Christians who found themselves at the mercy of Jews in business dealings.

CHECK THE FILM

The Oscar-winning Spielberg film *Schindler's List* (1993) gives an account of Jewish persecution under the Nazis and contains similar ideas at times to those in the play.

Now take a break!

WHO SAYS ...?

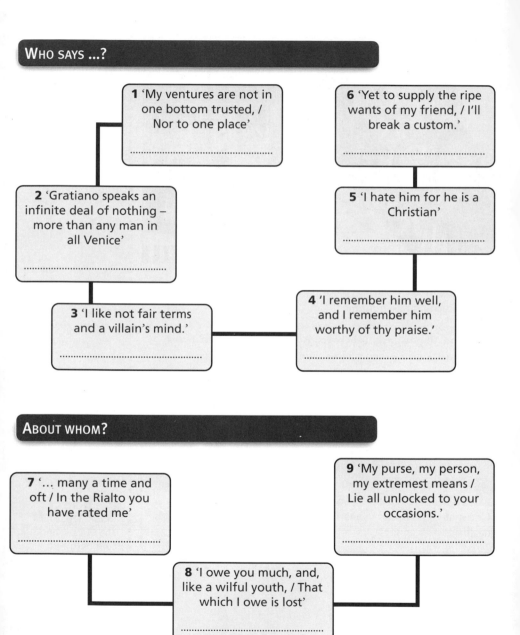

1 'My ventures are not in one bottom trusted, / Nor to one place'

....

2 'Gratiano speaks an infinite deal of nothing – more than any man in all Venice'

....

3 'I like not fair terms and a villain's mind.'

....

6 'Yet to supply the ripe wants of my friend, / I'll break a custom.'

....

5 'I hate him for he is a Christian'

....

4 'I remember him well, and I remember him worthy of thy praise.'

....

ABOUT WHOM?

7 '... many a time and oft / In the Rialto you have rated me'

....

8 'I owe you much, and, like a wilful youth, / That which I owe is lost'

....

9 'My purse, my person, my extremest means / Lie all unlocked to your occasions.'

....

Check your answers on p. 78.

SCENE 1 – Morocco prepares to take the test

1 **Portia and Morocco meet.**
2 **There is a terrible price to pay for taking the test of the caskets.**

Portia's house, Belmont. The Prince of Morocco is the latest in the line of Portia's suitors, and wishes to show his importance, his bravery and his wealth. Morocco challenges Portia to compare his blood to that of the fairest-skinned person in the world to 'prove whose blood is reddest, his or mine' (line 7). Skin colour was very important to the Elizabethans and this is one way of suggesting that Morocco is as noble as any white man.

The Prince is preparing to take the test of the caskets. Portia tells him that, if he fails, he must never 'speak to lady afterward / In way of marriage' (lines 41–2). Morocco agrees to these harsh terms.

SCENE 2 – Slapstick comedy – Launcelot and his father

1 **Launcelot amuses the audience at the expense of his father.**

Venice, near Shylock's house. Launcelot Gobbo is on stage by himself and gives an account of how he decided to leave Shylock's service. There then follows an absurd conversation between Launcelot and his father, Old Gobbo, in which the old man fails to recognise his son. Bassanio enters and is immediately approached by Old Gobbo, who wants a new position for his son. Bassanio agrees to take on Launcelot as his servant.

Gratiano enters and tells Bassanio that he wishes to go with him to Belmont. Bassanio agrees on condition Gratiano does not misbehave and so spoil his chance of courting Portia.

DID YOU KNOW?
Red blood signified courage and virility.

DID YOU KNOW?
Portia uses the word **'fair'** to mean both attractive and white-skinned.

CHECKPOINT 4

Sometimes Morocco is played as a man with great dignity. But there is ample scope in these lines for him to be played as a self-important fool. Explore both possibilities and see which you favour.

CHECKPOINT 5

Gobbo chooses the wrong word, a **malapropism**. What is this intended to show?

GLOSSARY

In way of marriage about marriage

DID YOU KNOW?

Shakespeare often uses the notion of mistaken identity in his plays. Sometimes it results in tragedy; sometimes, as in this play, it is used for comic effect.

Comic relief

This comic scene with Launcelot Gobbo occurs at the point where the audience want to see whether or not Morocco will choose the right casket. Comic scenes are often introduced to lighten the tone of the play and to keep the audience waiting.

Tension is built up then relaxed in this manner throughout the play. It would be too much to expect the audience to remain in a state of tension for three hours.

SCENE 3 – Jessica

❶ Jessica is unhappy.

Venice, Shylock's house. This is the first appearance of Jessica, Shylock's daughter. She tells Launcelot that she is sorry that he is leaving. More significantly, Jessica says that she is ashamed to be her father's child.

This short scene establishes that Jessica is unhappy and gives her a clear reason to leave her father. She is, of course, already in love with Lorenzo.

Even though she is Jewish, Jessica says that she wants to leave her father's faith and become a Christian.

DID YOU KNOW?

In Shakespeare's time Jews were encouraged, even forced, to give up their religion.

SCENE 4 – Planning to elope

❶ Lorenzo receives a letter from Jessica planning her escape.

Venice. Gratiano, Lorenzo, Salerio and Solanio are preparing to attend a masque, and discussing arrangements when Launcelot enters, bearing a letter from Jessica. It appears to be a love letter addressed to

Lorenzo, but after reading it, he announces that he does not need to look for a torchbearer for the evening, because Jessica is suggesting that she should disguise herself as his. Jessica is going to run away from her father and take some of his gold and jewels with her.

Jessica is prepared to steal from her own father. This would also cause him great pain, yet she seems quite ready to take his gold and jewels.

DID YOU KNOW?
In a Jewish family, the family line is passed on through the daughter.

Scene 5 – Jessica plans her escape

1 **Shylock tells Launcelot that he is free to go into Bassanio's service.**

2 **Jessica tells the audience that she is about to disown her father.**

Venice, Shylock's house. Shylock waits impatiently for Jessica. He has been invited to celebrate with the Christians but says, 'I am not bid for love; they flatter me; / But yet I'll go in hate' (lines 13–14).

Shylock has had a dream about moneybags and he thinks that this is a bad omen. He is also concerned that his house will be attacked by the young men of the city as they make their way to the masque.

Launcelot tells Jessica to look out of her window as Lorenzo is on his way to collect her. Launcelot interrupts Shylock throughout the scene. His unwitting comic remarks add to Shylock's growing frustration. Shylock goes, reluctantly, to the feast.

CHECKPOINT 6

Shylock has not noticed his daughter's recent odd behaviour. What does this tell you about him?

Scene 6 – The lovers elope: Bassanio heads for Belmont

1 **Jessica runs away from her father.**

2 **The wind changes for Belmont.**

Venice, outside Shylock's house. The young men are on their way to the masque. Gratiano and Salerio are waiting for Lorenzo who is late.

GLOSSARY
bid asked

Gratiano says that people in love are usually far too early. Jessica appears, on the balcony of her father's house, dressed as a page boy. She throws down to him much of Shylock's wealth saying 'Here, catch this casket; it is worth the pains' (line 33). Lorenzo and Jessica have planned to elope and they leave for the masque with the others.

? DID YOU KNOW?

Gratiano remarks that most things are better enjoyed when being chased than when you have them. Bear this in mind when he lands at Belmont.

CHECKPOINT 7

Bassanio gives up the expensive party very easily. What does this show about him?

Gratiano meets Antonio who brings word that the masque has been cancelled as the wind has changed direction and Bassanio can now set sail for Belmont.

Shakespeare's use of locations

We know that Belmont is some distance away from Venice. This means that it takes time for information and indeed for the characters to travel from one location to another.

This allows for the possibility of messages arriving late and characters missing one another in travelling to and fro. Shakespeare makes use of this on several occasions in the play. The first such instance is here with the ship's departure being delayed just long enough for the audience to become worried about the fate of Portia.

Scene 7 – Morocco takes the test

1 Morocco has to choose between caskets of gold, silver and lead.

2 Portia seems nervous about his taking the test.

3 Morocco chooses the wrong casket.

Belmont. Portia shows the Prince of Morocco to the caskets and asks him to make his choice. Morocco reads the inscription on each of the three caskets. They are:

● On the gold casket:
  'Who chooseth me shall gain what many men desire' (line 5).

● On the silver casket:
  'Who chooseth me shall get as much as he deserves' (line 7).

● On the lead casket:
  'Who chooseth me must give and hazard all he hath' (line 16).

Portia tells him that one of the caskets contains her picture. If he chooses the right one then she will be his. Morocco takes a very long time to decide. He dismisses the lead casket as he thinks that lead is

CHECKPOINT 8

Why does Shakespeare deliberately delay Morocco's choice?

not worth hazarding all for, the silver casket, which does not appear grand enough to signify Portia, and eventually settles upon the gold because it is the most precious and promises to deliver 'what many men desire' (line 5). Morocco takes this to mean Portia. He looks at each of the caskets again before deciding. Finally, he chooses the gold, but the gold holds only a 'carrion Death' (line 63) and, sticking out of one of the eye sockets, a scroll on which is written a nine–line poem, pointing out that Morocco has chosen foolishly. The poem begins '*All that glisters is not gold*' (line 65). Portia is glad that he made the wrong choice.

DID YOU KNOW?

The first line of the poem is often quoted. It is a warning that things are not always what they seem.

The test of the caskets

This is not one of Shakespeare's own ideas. The four main elements of the plot of *The Merchant of Venice* were well-known stories in 1598 when the play was entered in the Stationer's Register. Some were Italian stories of the sixteenth century whilst the episode of the caskets originated in medieval tales.

Though Shakespeare borrowed from these various sources, he changed them sufficiently to suit his own dramatic purposes.

A key question is whether Portia secretly knows which casket is which and whether she has been so devious as to 'rig' the outcome.

CHECK THE NET

Examine the likely sources of the tale used in the play at **www.shakespeare-online.com**

A prince's word was not something that he could break. A man's reputation rested on his word.

Portia's final remark is a reference to Morocco's personality, but also to his skin colour. To a modern audience, Portia may well become a less sympathetic character because of her reaction to the idea of marrying a man with dark skin.

SCENE 8 – Shylock's anger; bad news for Antonio

1 Shylock is upset and annoyed at Jessica's disappearance with his money.

2 One of Antonio's ships might have been lost.

Venice. Salerio and Solanio are discussing the departure of Bassanio's ship. Shylock had attempted to have the ship searched in order to find Lorenzo and Jessica. The ship had already sailed, but there have been reports that Lorenzo and Jessica have been seen together in a gondola. Shylock is beside himself with a mixture of anger and grief. He does not seem to know whether it is the loss of his daughter or the loss of his money that upsets him most. He has been heard to cry 'My daughter! O my ducats! O my daughter!' (line 15).

News has reached Venice that a Venetian ship has run aground in the English Channel. Solanio hopes that it is not one of Antonio's ships.

Salerio reports that, although Antonio is in debt to Shylock, he has told Bassanio not to rush his wooing of Portia and so lessen his chances of success. Antonio has told his friend not to think of the bond made with the Jew. Salerio and Solanio set off to look for Antonio.

Note the attitude of these two men towards Shylock. Clearly they see him as a figure of fun and are pleased that he has suffered, yet they would describe themselves as Christians. In addition, Antonio is extremely kind to his friend. This contrasts sharply with his treatment of Shylock.

The role of minor characters

Minor characters are often used to update the audience on recent events. This allows the plot to move along more swiftly.

Salerio and Solanio along with Launcelot are used on several occasions to fill in gaps in the narrative. They also serve to highlight the attitudes of ordinary people of the day, in this case towards Jews.

CHECKPOINT 9

What are we meant to think about this ship?

GLOSSARY
carrion Death a skull
ducats gold coins

SCENE 9 – The Prince of Arragon

❶ **Arragon arrives to take the test.**

❷ **He chooses the silver casket and fails.**

Belmont, a room in Portia's house. The Prince of Arragon has arrived
to take the test of the caskets. Portia shows him to them and explains
the conditions attached. They are:

- He must never reveal to anyone the casket which he chose

- If he chooses wrongly, he may never ask a woman to marry him

- If he chooses wrongly, he must leave at once

 **DID YOU
KNOW?**

Ar(r)agon was an
ancient kingdom of
north-east Spain.
England and Spain
were great rivals at
the time the play
was written.

Arragon does a great deal of deliberating about which casket he
should choose. He reasons that the message on the gold casket makes
it too common for him to choose. He finally settles upon the silver
one as he feels that he deserves Portia. (See **Summary** on **Act II Scene
7** for an explanation of the message with each casket.) When he opens
the casket he finds a portrait of a blinking idiot, and an accompanying
rhyme telling him that he is a fool and ending with '*So be gone, you
are sped*' (line 72).

Arragon leaves, but before Nerissa can draw the curtain on the caskets
a messenger arrives and says that another lord has arrived. The new
arrival is Venetian and his companion (Gratiano) is described as 'So
likely an ambassador of love' (line 92).

Portia obviously hopes that the latest visitor is Bassanio. Shakespeare
does not reveal this yet, thus developing dramatic tension.

Now take a break!

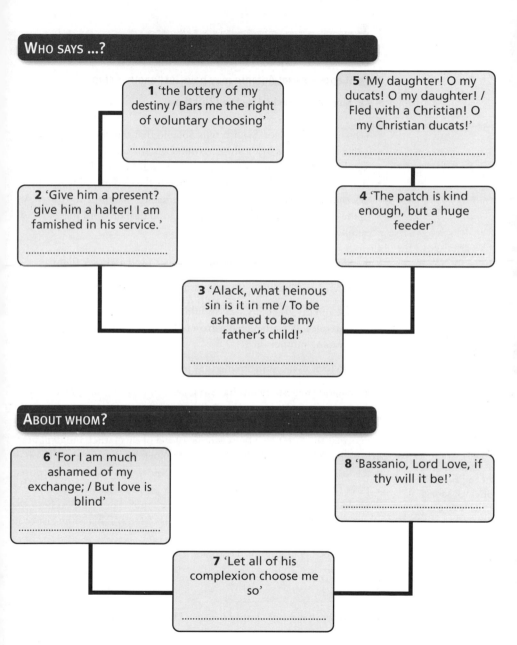

WHO SAYS ...?

1 'the lottery of my destiny / Bars me the right of voluntary choosing'

....

5 'My daughter! O my ducats! O my daughter! / Fled with a Christian! O my Christian ducats!'

....

2 'Give him a present? give him a halter! I am famished in his service.'

....

4 'The patch is kind enough, but a huge feeder'

....

3 'Alack, what heinous sin is it in me / To be ashamed to be my father's child!'

....

ABOUT WHOM?

6 'For I am much ashamed of my exchange; / But love is blind'

....

8 'Bassanio, Lord Love, if thy will it be!'

....

7 'Let all of his complexion choose me so'

....

Check your answers on p. 78.

SCENE 1 – Antonio's ships: Shylock's despair

❶ **It appears that Antonio may have lost another ship.**

❷ **Shylock is mocked by the Christians.**

Venice, a public place. Salerio tells Solanio that the news in the Rialto is that Antonio has lost a ship, aground on 'the Goodwins' (line 4). Salerio and Solanio act as narrators, as they did in Act II Scene 8. Shylock enters and immediately confronts the two men. He is sure that they knew very well that his daughter was planning to run away. In the exchange that follows there is a good deal of word play, as outlined below:

- Shylock accuses them of knowledge of his daughter's flight

- Salerio says he knew the tailor that made her wings

- Solanio says that Shylock should have known that a bird leaves its nest once its feathers have grown. He uses the word 'dam' (line 29) meaning mother bird

- Shylock uses a **pun** saying that Jessica is damned for it

- Salerio suggests again that Shylock is 'the devil' (line 19)

Shylock keeps referring to Jessica as his flesh and blood, but Salerio says that the difference between the blood of this father and daughter is like that between black and white. Shylock has heard the news of the loss of Antonio's ship. He calls Antonio a waster and then repeats three times that the merchant must 'look to his bond' (line 43). Shylock then delivers one of Shakespeare's most famous speeches opening with 'Hath not a Jew eyes?' (lines 54–69). This is the gist of it:

- Shylock is intent upon revenge.

- He recounts all the times that Antonio has insulted him and his friends.

- Antonio did this simply because Shylock was a Jew.

- A Jew is a man like any other. He feels the same things.

DID YOU KNOW?

Yet again, Shylock is referred to as the devil.

DID YOU KNOW?

This close repetition of the bond makes Shylock sound calculating and menacing.

● Christians exact revenge when they are wronged, so why shouldn't a Jew do the same?

● The Christian, Antonio, will be treated as he treats others.

A servant brings a message that Antonio is looking for Salerio and Solanio. Tubal, a rich Jew, enters and Solanio comments again that the Jews can only be matched by the devil himself. Tubal and Shylock are left onstage and Tubal gives an account of Jessica's movements and action since running away.

Shylock's sadness at the loss of his daughter is mixed with despair at the loss of his wealth. He even says that he wishes Jessica were dead at his feet along with the jewels which she has stolen. Tubal tells Shylock that he has heard in Genoa that Antonio has lost a ship near Tripoli in North Africa. Shylock is overjoyed at the news. Shylock vows to have the heart of Antonio if he breaks the terms of the bond. Shylock swears to take revenge upon Antonio for Jessica's behaviour, though Antonio is not actually responsible for this.

Tubal also tells of the way in which Jessica has been spending her father's money carelessly: eighty ducats in one evening. Jessica has exchanged a ring which Shylock values greatly, for a monkey.

The ring is of sentimental value to Shylock and, here, Jessica seems to have gone too far in her humiliation of her father, even though she may not have known of the ring's importance.

The use of prose

Much of the argument takes place in **prose**. This is unusual for major speeches such as Shylock's, lines 49–69. This can be seen as having two effects:

● It makes Shylock appear to be more human as he is not always completely in control.

● Shylock seems perhaps to be less noble here than at other times in the play.

See **Language and style** for more discussion.

CHECKPOINT 10

Is Tubal gloating or truly sympathetic towards Antonio here?

 DID YOU KNOW?

As the ring means a great deal to Shylock it is likely that Leah was his wife.

 DID YOU KNOW?

Shylock's speech, lines 49–69 contains many ideas taken straight from the teachings of the Christian Church. He is using the Christians' own arguments against them.

GLOSSARY

the Goodwins a dangerous sandbank in the Straits of Dover

dam mother

SCENE 2 – Bassanio and the caskets

1 Portia asks Bassanio to wait for a few days before making the choice of the caskets.

2 Bassanio wishes to take the test immediately.

3 Bassanio hears bad news about Antonio.

Belmont, Portia's house. Portia says that she wishes she could tell Bassanio which casket to pick, but that she cannot. She is bound by the terms of her father's will. Portia realises that she has said too much, but adds that she is happy to talk as long as it puts off the moment when Bassanio might have to take the test. Bassanio says that waiting is like being tortured upon the rack.

Portia tells Bassanio to take the test. She trusts that his love will lead him to choose the casket containing her picture. Portia compares her situation to that of Hesione, a beautiful young woman of Troy, who was to be sacrificed to a sea monster. Hercules rescued her and killed the monster. There is then some music whilst Bassanio examines the caskets. Look at the way that Shakespeare keeps Portia and the audience waiting even though the outcome is not really in doubt. This is to develop tension.

DID YOU KNOW?

The rack was an instrument of torture, used to make people confess to treason.

CHECKPOINT 11

Think about whether Portia really considers herself to be a victim.

In the first line of his speech, lines 73–107, Bassanio makes the comment 'So may the outward shows be least themselves'. He then makes the points:

- Evil deeds are often explained away by citing a passage of scripture.

- Cowards may grow beards to show that they are brave, but their livers are still white.

- Beauty can be bought in the form of cosmetics, but the person who uses them the most is likely to be the least beautiful.

- Curly, long, blond hair was considered beautiful, but many who appeared to have such hair were in fact wearing wigs made from the hair of corpses.

- A beautiful scarf might hide dark skin. (The Elizabethans found dark skin unattractive.)

Bassanio discounts the caskets of gold and silver and chooses the casket of lead. Portia is delighted at his decision and says that she can think of nothing else. She then tells him that she is really just an ordinary woman and not the fantastic creature he has just made her out to be. Portia says that everything she has, including herself, now belongs to Bassanio whom she calls 'her lord, her governor, her king' (line 165). She gives him a ring as a token of her love. Gratiano announces that he and Nerissa have fallen in love and wish to be married.

> ### Portia the woman
>
> Portia is much less assured when speaking to Bassanio than to her previous suitors. She is nervous because she wants him to choose correctly and, more so, because, perhaps, she knows which casket he should choose.
>
> We know Portia to be very strong-willed, yet she readily gives herself to Bassanio as if she were something he had just bought. Her use of the words 'lord ... governor ... king ...' (line 165) suggest that she is a more conventional woman than she has previously made herself out to be.

CHECKPOINT 12

Is it possible that Portia knows which casket contains her portrait? Would this make her more, or less, nervous?

 DID YOU KNOW?
A white liver was thought to indicate cowardice.

CHECKPOINT 13

Note Portia's change of attitude towards men and humble opinion of herself. What might this signify?

DID YOU KNOW?

Portia's speech, lines 40–62, ends in a **rhyming couplet**. This is unusual within a scene and tells us that something important is to happen.

Lorenzo, Jessica, Salerio and a messenger from Venice enter. Bassanio is given a letter from Antonio which says that all the merchant's ventures have failed due to disaster at sea. Salerio says that Shylock is determined to have his pound of flesh; no one in Venice has been able to persuade him to change his mind. Portia offers to give Shylock much more money than he is owed and asks Bassanio to take it to Venice.

Bassanio praises Portia rather too much. This could be due to his joy at winning her hand, yet also shows that he is trying too hard to be sincere.

Scene 3 – Antonio is imprisoned

❶ Shylock insists that Antonio is imprisoned.

DID YOU KNOW?

As in Act III Scene 1, Shylock repeats a phrase about the bond. At this point, he is obsessive and beyond all reason.

Venice, a street. Shylock instructs a jailer to imprison Antonio. The merchant tries to get Shylock to listen to him but the Jew is set upon revenge and will not listen to anyone. Antonio realises that Shylock wishes to kill him. He thinks, however, that this is because he has often released people from their debts to Shylock and makes no mention of his own appalling behaviour over the years.

Not even the Duke of Venice can break the terms of the bond. Venice would lose its reputation as an honest trading centre if the Duke broke his own laws.

Scene 4 – Portia has a plan

❶ Portia sends to her cousin, a lawyer, for help.

❷ The wives (Portia and Nerissa) are to dress as lawyers and go to Venice.

Belmont. Lorenzo praises Portia's generosity telling her that she has noble and a true conceit' (line 2) and would be even prouder of her actions if she knew what a true gentleman Antonio was. Portia replies that she is sure Antonio must be very like Bassanio as the two are such close friends. She entrusts her house to Lorenzo and says that she and Nerissa will live in a monastery until the return of their husbands.

There is hardly any conversation between Portia and Jessica. This is in contrast to the sudden closeness formed between Portia and Bassanio and Nerissa and Gratiano.

Portia sends her servant, Balthazar, to Padua with a note for her cousin Doctor Bellario. Balthazar is to take whatever documents and clothing he is given to Venice as quickly as he can. Portia tells Nerissa that they will 'see our husbands / Before they think of us' (lines 58–9). The two women are to go to Venice dressed as men.

Portia, lines 60–78, gives an amusing account of the typical behaviour of young men.

On two occasions, lines 61–2 and 79–80, Portia makes sexually explicit jokes to Nerissa. This shows her to be a little more worldly-wise than she might at first seem.

CHECKPOINT 14

What do these plans show of Portia's character?

SCENE 5 – Comic relief with Launcelot

❶ Jessica becomes a Christian.

Launcelot tells Jessica that he fears she is damned because she is the daughter of a Jew. She announces that her husband, Lorenzo, has made her a Christian. Lorenzo accuses Launcelot of having got a black girl pregnant. This is all dismissed as a joke. Launcelot plays upon words to the point that he becomes irritating. The lovers discuss Portia, and Lorenzo comments that he is as much to be admired as Portia is. This is an odd thing for Lorenzo to say. He seems to have a very high opinion of himself, though he may be simply making a joke.

This scene is another example of comedy being used to lighten the feel of the play. In practical terms it allows Portia to dress for the next scene.

DID YOU KNOW?

Christians felt only they could go to heaven.

GLOSSARY

conceit understanding

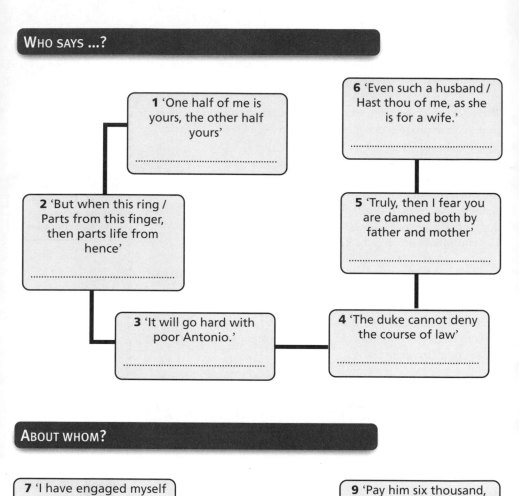

Who says ...?

1 'One half of me is yours, the other half yours'

....

2 'But when this ring / Parts from this finger, then parts life from hence'

....

3 'It will go hard with poor Antonio.'

....

6 'Even such a husband / Hast thou of me, as she is for a wife.'

....

5 'Truly, then I fear you are damned both by father and mother'

....

4 'The duke cannot deny the course of law'

....

About whom?

7 'I have engaged myself to a dear friend'

....

8 'Thou call'dst me dog before thou hadst a cause'

....

9 'Pay him six thousand, and deface the bond'

....

Check your answers on p. 78

SCENE 1 – The trial

1 Shylock insists on having his bond.

2 Portia and Nerissa arrive dressed as lawyers.

3 Portia outwits Shylock.

4 Shylock is punished.

Venice, the Duke's Palace. The Duke expresses his sympathy for Antonio, but Antonio says there is nothing more the Duke can do if Shylock remains determined. Shylock is summoned and the Duke pleads with him to show mercy saying 'We all expect a gentle answer, Jew!' (line 34).

Shylock stands by his promise to take the pound of flesh. He points out that if the Duke denies him his legal rights, the whole charter of the City of Venice will be worthless. Shylock refuses to explain himself and simply says that it pleases him to have a pound of Antonio's flesh. Despite Bassanio's attempts to reason with Shylock, he will not change his mind.

Antonio resigns himself to his fate with 'Let me have judgement, and the Jew his will' (line 84). Bassanio offers the Jew twice the money he is owed but Shylock says he would not accept even six times the debt.

Nerissa enters, disguised as a lawyer's clerk and gives the Duke a letter from the learned Doctor Bellario. Gratiano makes a vicious verbal attack upon Shylock calling him 'damned, inexorable dog' (line 128) but Shylock still refuses to change his mind. Portia enters, disguised as Doctor Balthazar, and appeals to Shylock for mercy. Shylock insists on the law being upheld, even after Portia offers him the money three times. Portia says that Shylock is quite entitled under the law to cut off a pound of Antonio's flesh and Shylock thinks that the lawyer is as wise as Daniel. Portia asks for a surgeon to be brought to stop Antonio from bleeding to death but Shylock will not allow this as it is not stated in the terms of the bond. Antonio prepares to die and Bassanio says that even though he has just married, he would gladly give himself, his wife and all the world to save Antonio.

EXAMINER'S SECRET

Imagine the expressions of the actors as they listen to Portia setting a trap for Shylock. Try to convey the sense of drama experienced by a real audience.

CHECKPOINT 15

How is Portia setting a trap for Shylock?

GLOSSARY

inexorable cursed beyond redemption

DID YOU KNOW?

Portia's speech about the quality of mercy is very famous.

DID YOU KNOW?

Shakespeare sets up the next element of the plot even at such a crucial moment.

Portia adds that his wife would not thank him for making such an offer and Gratiano announces that he wishes his wife were dead so that she could plead with God to make Shylock change his mind.

Shylock is about to cut into Antonio's flesh when Portia stops him. She points out that the bond allows him to take a pound of flesh, but does not mention shedding one drop of blood. Antonio is saved.

Portia then pursues Shylock by insisting upon the following:

- Shylock shall have only his bond. He cannot now decide to take the money which he earlier refused.

- By attempting to kill a Christian, Shylock has broken the laws of Venice.

- Under these laws, the victim (Antonio) is due half of Shylock's wealth and the state of Venice the other half.

- In addition, Shylock's life is in the hands of the Duke.

Antonio gives his half of Shylock's goods to Lorenzo and Jessica as a wedding present. He then insists that Shylock convert to Christianity and make Lorenzo and Jessica beneficiaries of his will.

CHECKPOINT 16

Does Antonio go too far here, bearing in mind what Portia has already done?

Portia says she will take no money for her services, but insists that Bassanio should give her his ring, which he does. This troubles him greatly as he has promised never to part with it. Portia is using the ring to test her husband. She may also be interested to see whether he puts his loyalty to Antonio before his loyalty to her.

Justice in England (and Venice)

Shakespeare's portrayal of the laws of Venice is really just an adaptation of the laws of England in the sixteenth century. Such laws allowed non-Christians very few rights and were aimed at protecting the wealthy.

Shylock is quite entitled to take a pound of flesh. He insists that he is acting lawfully but fails to see that the law is intended to be just.

The same Christians who think Shylock is unjust keep slaves. The law allows this and so they think it is acceptable. Shakespeare seems keen to point out the strange morality of despising moneylenders yet supporting slavery.

The laws regarding an 'alien' (line 345) plotting the murder of a citizen apply to Shylock because he is Jewish. A Christian would not receive such harsh treatment.

SCENE 2 – The rings – the wives test their new husbands

1 **Portia and Nerissa, in disguise, get their rings from their husbands.**

A street in Venice. Portia sends Nerissa to find Shylock's house. Nerissa is to ask Shylock to sign a deed naming Lorenzo and Jessica as his heirs. Gratiano brings Bassanio's ring to Portia and Nerissa thinks it would be amusing to try to get Gratiano to part with the ring that she has given him. Portia says that the two women will turn old

CHECK THE BOOK
Schindler's Ark by Thomas Keneally (1983), on which the film *Schindler's List* (1993) was based, tells the story of a man who helped Jews to escape from the Nazis.

CHECKPOINT 17

How does the plot change here?

Scene 2 continued

EXAMINER'S SECRET

Always read the whole examination paper before you start writing.

listening to their husbands swearing that they gave the rings away to men but will 'outface them, and outswear them too' (line 17).

Portia moves very quickly from pursuing Shylock to arranging an elaborate practical joke. Clearly the fate of Shylock does not trouble her conscience in the slightest.

Wives, husbands and rings

Once Portia has defeated Shylock that element of the plot is over. In order for the play to regain a lighter tone after the serious moments in the courtroom, Shakespeare introduces a new plot. This is to revolve around the idea of wives testing their husband's loyalties.

Portia has revealed a conventional side to her nature (in Elizabethan terms) by promising to give herself completely to Bassanio. Here we see the stronger side of Portia's nature as she prepares for Nerissa and herself to outwit their new husbands. Portia reveals that she is:

- Witty

- Imaginative

- Cruel

The play moves from potential tragedy to light humour. It is at this point that *The Merchant of Venice* becomes a tragi-comedy.

Now take a break!

WHO SAYS ...?

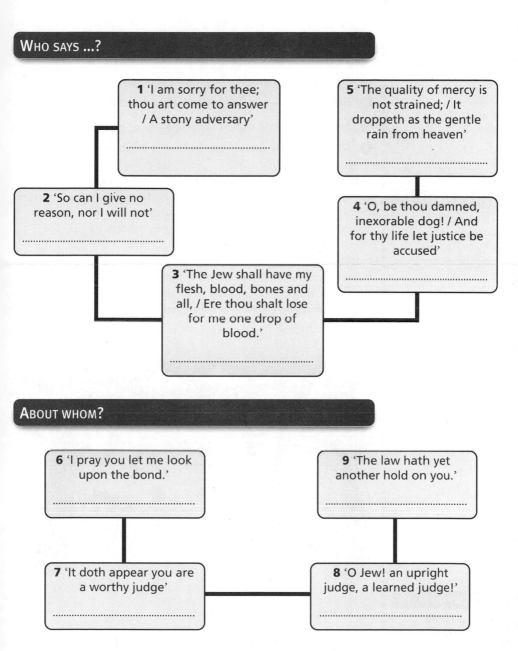

1 'I am sorry for thee; thou art come to answer / A stony adversary'

....

2 'So can I give no reason, nor I will not'

....

3 'The Jew shall have my flesh, blood, bones and all, / Ere thou shalt lose for me one drop of blood.'

....

5 'The quality of mercy is not strained; / It droppeth as the gentle rain from heaven'

....

4 'O, be thou damned, inexorable dog! / And for thy life let justice be accused'

....

ABOUT WHOM?

6 'I pray you let me look upon the bond.'

....

7 'It doth appear you are a worthy judge'

....

9 'The law hath yet another hold on you.'

....

8 'O Jew! an upright judge, a learned judge!'

....

Check your answers on p. 78

SCENE 1 – Resolution

❶ Portia pretends that she has not left Belmont.

❷ The husbands are forced to admit they gave their rings away.

❸ Portia and Nerissa exploit the situation.

❹ All ends happily (unless you happen to be Shylock).

CHECKPOINT 18

What part do
Lorenzo and
Jessica play here?

Belmont, Portia's garden. Lorenzo and Jessica are interrupted by the arrival of Stephano, bringing news that Portia will arrive home before dawn. She has been delayed as she has taken time to pray at several holy shrines. Launcelot stumbles around in the dark looking for Lorenzo, finds him and announces that Bassanio is also due home before daybreak. Lorenzo arranges for music to be played to welcome home Portia and Bassanio. Lorenzo links this to the belief that the stars in the heavens made music when they moved. He believes in the power of music to create atmosphere and feels that gentle music can calm the wildest beast.

CHECKPOINT 19

What is Portia
plotting here?

Portia and Nerissa enter and are drawn into the romantic atmosphere created by the music. When the music stops the characters become much more straightforward in the way they talk. Portia finds out that

Bassanio and Gratiano have not yet arrived and gives orders that no one should mention that the women have also been away.

The husbands arrive with Antonio. Bassanio immediately flatters Portia, saying that she is like the sun to him. She makes a sexually explicit joke, then remembers herself and greets Antonio. Nerissa has challenged Gratiano as to why he is not wearing the ring she gave him, and accuses him of having given it to a woman – which, of course, he has. Portia joins in the telling off and, to make Gratiano feel worse, says that she gave a ring to Bassanio but that he would never have given his away. Gratiano swears that Bassanio gave his ring to the judge whilst he gave his to the clerk. Portia adds to her husband's discomfort by saying that she will never sleep with him until she has seen the ring and Nerissa promises the same to Gratiano. Bassanio begs Portia to believe that he has not given the ring to a woman; the joke is that he has. Bassanio could lie about the loss of the ring, yet he chooses to tell Portia the truth. This is a little unexpected, as we have not seen this side of his character before.

? DID YOU KNOW?
At this point, Portia has not yet slept with her husband.

? DID YOU KNOW?
The terms lawyer, doctor and judge are used to mean the same thing here.

The situation is taken one stage further when Portia insists 'I'll have that doctor for my bedfellow' (line 233). She cannot do anything else since she is, in fact, the lawyer. Nerissa makes a similar pronouncement and Antonio feels that he must intervene to support his friends. At this, Portia produces Bassanio's ring and says that she

? DID YOU KNOW?
All of the elements of the plot have been neatly tied up.

CHECK THE NET

for 'Adreas Capellanus' who wrote about the rules of courtly love in the thirteenth century.

received it from the doctor after having slept with him. The men are amazed at their wives' behaviour. Portia finally lets them off the hook by giving them a letter from Doctor Bellario explaining that she had been the lawyer and Nerissa her clerk. She also gives Antonio a letter which tells him that three of his ships have arrived safely. Portia may have known all along that Antonio's ships had arrived safely. It is difficult to explain from where she suddenly produced the letter that she gives to Antonio. If she did know, then the whole trial scene was allowed to take place, purely for Portia's benefit.

> **Courtly love**
>
> The characters behave in a manner dictated by the idea of courtly love. This convention (set of unwritten rules) demanded that lovers spoke and acted in certain ways.
>
> Lorenzo and Jessica speak like typical lovers. Note the repetition of the phrase 'In such a night', (lines 1, 6, 9, 12, 14 and so on). The stories they tell, however, such as 'Troilus' (line 4) and 'Cressid' (line 6), and 'Dido' (line 10) deal with tragedy and betrayal. This seems unusually gloomy for two newly weds.
>
> The conversations between the two couples are full of sexual innuendo. They almost forget themselves and embarrass their guests.

The couples retire to bed after further joking from Gratiano.

The play is given a rather silly, happy ending in keeping with Shakespeare's intention for it to be a comedy. It is interesting to consider what Shylock might be doing at this point.

GLOSSARY

Troilus and **Cressid** Troilus was betrayed by his lover, Cressid(a)

Dido Queen of Carthage, abandoned by her lover

WHO SAYS ...?

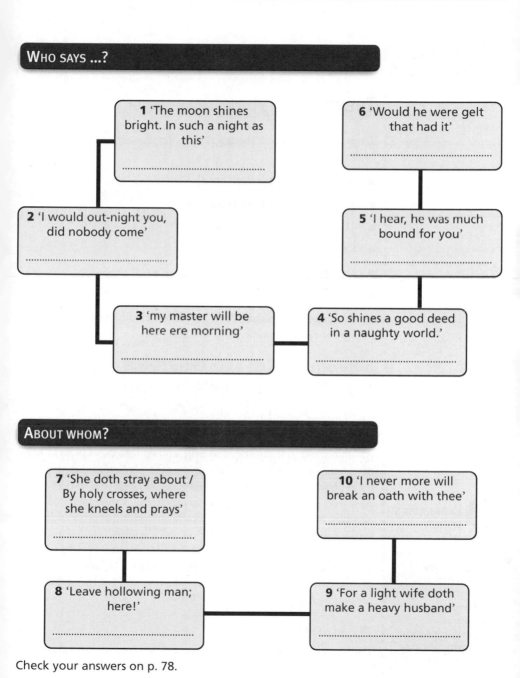

1 'The moon shines bright. In such a night as this'

....

2 'I would out-night you, did nobody come'

....

3 'my master will be here ere morning'

....

6 'Would he were gelt that had it'

....

5 'I hear, he was much bound for you'

....

4 'So shines a good deed in a naughty world.'

....

ABOUT WHOM?

7 'She doth stray about / By holy crosses, where she kneels and prays'

....

8 'Leave hollowing man; here!'

....

10 'I never more will break an oath with thee'

....

9 'For a light wife doth make a heavy husband'

....

Check your answers on p. 78.

PART THREE

COMMENTARY

THEMES

There are several major themes in *The Merchant of Venice*. They could be described as:

- Bonds that exist between people

- True justice as opposed to the law

- The importance of marriage

- Revenge

- First appearances can be deceptive

- The sea

All the themes are linked to the ways in which different people respond to the environments in which they live.

BONDS THAT EXIST BETWEEN PEOPLE

There are three clear examples of different types of bond in the play.

The bond of friendship

From the very first scene in which Bassanio reveals that he is tied to Antonio through friendship and debt, and Antonio says that the bond of friendship between them cancels the debt, Shakespeare explores the bond between friends. This is tested when Shylock tries to take Antonio's life. Antonio's sacrifice for his friend is an example of altruism. He can be very generous to his friend and yet treat others badly. Bassanio offers to change places with Antonio so that his friend will not be harmed. The loyalty of friendship is further tested by Portia when she demands the ring from Bassanio. Because of the debt of loyalty that Bassanio owes her for the rescue of his friend, he has to break the promise that he made to his wife.

The bond of hatred

The bond of hatred between Shylock and Antonio is a central element of the play. It is this which leads to the actual bond of the pound of

EXAMINER'S SECRET

Try producing a single revision sheet for each of the key characters and themes. Set it out in the form of a diagram with essential quotations and **some phrases of your own**.

flesh being signed. Antonio and Shylock seem strangely bound together as they are unable to avoid one another. There is no mention of other Christians hating Shylock as strongly as Antonio does and Tubal does not report any such problem.

Family bonds

The bond of family is the third type we meet. Jessica decides that she is more strongly tied to Lorenzo than to her own father. The play also raises questions here as to whether she should have to make this choice at all. Launcelot and Gobbo are not close, even though they are father and son. Portia's father's will shows his concern to find her a husband who will not marry her just for her wealth. Portia obeys her father's will though there is little other than a promise keeping her to it. These different strengths of family relationship are key issues in *The Merchant of Venice*.

LAW VERSUS JUSTICE

The link between the law and justice is explored thoroughly. It is clear from the behaviour of:

- Antonio towards Shylock

- Shylock when seeking revenge

- Portia when punishing Shylock

- Antonio when insisting Shylock convert to Christianity

- The Duke who lets events follow the law

that the law in Venice is not capable of providing justice. Portia's famous speech asks for justice and mercy, yet she does not show Shylock any such justice when she insists on his punishment. The play questions submission to a law which people know to be unjust.

QUESTIONING THE VOWS OF MARRIAGE

The strength of marriage vows is questioned through the plots involving Portia and Bassanio, Nerissa and Gratiano, and Jessica and Lorenzo. At this time, many wealthy people had their marriages arranged by their parents. Portia's father has taken this one step further by dictating the terms of his daughter's marriage from beyond

DID YOU KNOW?

The Royal Shakespeare Company's 1987 production with Antony Sher as Shylock featured swastikas and anti-Semitic propaganda scrawled on the walls of Venice.

the grave. The vows of marriage are examined through the three couples and the following picture emerges:

- Two of the husbands break their vows at the first hurdle.

- Lorenzo and Jessica are not fully accepted as a couple.

Bassanio is tied to Antonio and there is the question of what Antonio will do now that his best friend is married. Jessica has betrayed her father and her religion and so is not portrayed as having the happy future she would have wished for.

CHECK THE NET

Find out about marriage in Elizabethan England at **www.renaissance. dm.net**

In the play, friendship certainly seems to produce a stronger kind of loyalty than marriage.

REVENGE

Revenge occurs in various degrees throughout the play. The following are examples of revenge:

- Shylock attempts to kill Antonio

- Portia punishes Shylock

- Antonio makes Shylock convert

- Portia and Nerissa trick their husbands then watch them try to explain

FIRST APPEARANCES CAN BE DECEPTIVE

The idea of appearances not being what they seem is another important theme of the play. Portia makes up her mind about her suitors after only having met them briefly. In the case of Morocco, she gives an opinion of him before she has even seen him. Paradoxically, Bassanio is very keen on appearances!

The two failed suitors, Morocco and Arragon made the mistake of choosing a casket based on outward appearances. The rhyme which Morocco finds in the casket is particularly appropriate to this theme.

The lovers seem to have made the decision to marry based on appearances. They cannot have known one another for long and the caskets serve as a warning to them that they might live to regret their decisions.

THE SEA

Finally, there is a background theme of life on the high seas. The plot pivots on this: had Antonio's merchant ships travelled safely, Shylock would not have been able to demand revenge. The play is full of sea **imagery**, and an English audience would have enjoyed all this familiar sea lore.

DID YOU KNOW?

England was a major seafaring nation at the time of the play and tales of the sea were common.

STRUCTURE

The play divides into several areas of plot and location. The plots running through the play are:

- Antonio and Shylock: the pound of flesh

- Portia and the caskets: who will win Portia's hand?

- Lorenzo and Jessica: betrayal and elopement

- Portia and Bassanio/Nerissa and Gratiano: the rings used as a test of loyalty

These plots take place either in Venice or in Belmont.

CREATING SUSPENSE

In *The Merchant of Venice,* Shakespeare creates moments of great suspense. Much of the way he does this is through his manner of switching between plots and locations at vital points in the proceedings. Consider the following examples of the audience being kept in suspense:

In Act I Scene 2 we learn that Portia must marry whichever man chooses the right casket. At the end of the scene the arrival of the Prince of Morocco is announced, but we have to wait whilst Shylock and Antonio agree the bond before we are taken back to Portia. Even then, in Act II Scene 1, we do not see Morocco make his choice. We have to wait until Act II Scene 7 for this. By the time Morocco

CHECKPOINT 20

Why does Shakespeare set the play in several different locations?

chooses the gold casket, another plot has been introduced: the planned elopement of Jessica with Lorenzo. Look at the **Table of events** on p. 10 and see how this develops through Acts I and II.

Shakespeare weaves the different plots together, never spending so much time on one that we forget about the others. Switching between plots in this way is used today in a good deal of television drama, particularly in soap operas.

Sometimes the audience is ahead of the characters, such as in the episode with the rings. On other occasions the audience is not shown something until the characters themselves see it, as in the choice of the caskets. By varying the use of these techniques, Shakespeare is able to develop both humour and dramatic tension.

CHARACTERS

ANTONIO

Antonio's position is high in the social order of Venice. He is not actually a member of the aristocracy and so can never have the power that the Duke exercises, but he is a wealthy and well-known merchant, with all of the influence that money brings. The behaviour of Salerio and Solanio tells us that Antonio's friendship is a useful thing to have. A wealthy person who takes someone under his wing is known as a **patron**, and Antonio behaves as Bassanio's patron.

Though Antonio would have called himself a Christian, he has a vicious side to him. He knows that the law will support him if he persecutes the Jews and Antonio does not have the moral strength to resist acting like a bully. Just as many ordinary Germans allowed themselves to be swept along by the anti-Semitism of the Nazis, Antonio has been affected by the thinking of the time in which he lived. Shakespeare's audience would not have seen Antonio's actions as being unjust; they would have expected to see the Jew being punished.

Wealthy and well known

Loyal friend

Morally weak

Bully, hiding behind a bad law

At the end of the trial scene, it is Antonio who presses for the full punishment of Shylock. Considering that only moments before, his own life had been in danger, you might expect Antonio to show some mercy. He does not; instead he seeks revenge. Antonio's behaviour is really no better than Shylock's, but because Antonio is a Christian, the laws of Venice support him.

DID YOU KNOW?
Antonio's attitude to Shylock never changes, even when Antonio is at the mercy of the Jew.

He is not a simple character. His appalling treatment of Shylock contrasts sharply with his strong loyalty to Bassanio. Antonio is, quite literally, prepared to die for his friend. The close relationship he has with Bassanio is often puzzling to a modern audience. Men would have spent a great deal of time together without any women being around and this has certainly been the case with Antonio and Bassanio. Antonio does not seem comfortable in the presence of Portia when they meet in Act V and there is no mention of Antonio wishing to find a wife.

PORTIA

Portia is a very strong character. Shakespeare often portrays women as being cleverer and more resourceful than men, and this play is no exception. Like all interesting characters, however, Portia has a dark side. In Act I Scene 2 she is first portrayed as a victim, helplessly bound by the will of her dead father. She then goes on to give a witty account of each of her most recent suitors, showing the Elizabethan bigoted attitude towards foreigners. When she first speaks of the Prince of Morocco, Portia talks of him having 'the complexion of a devil' (I.2.124).

Later, in Act II Scene 7, she says: 'Let all of his complexion choose me so' (II.7.79) . This remark is clearly a reference to the colour of Morocco's skin, only here it is not made purely as a joke. She is no less racist than many of the men in the play.

Having seen Portia being strong, witty and racist, we then see her change completely once Bassanio has chosen the correct casket. She gives a very modest account of herself and immediately tells Bassanio that she is his to command as he is now her 'king' (III.2.165). This does not fit in with the sharp-tongued woman who gave such a harsh description of her suitors, unless she was simply 'acting tough' in order to put out of her mind the terrible prospect of marrying one of them. We might have expected Portia to keep Bassanio waiting, but

Loyal to father
Very intelligent
Mischievous and witty
Capable of cruelty

she marries him at once. In some ways she is a far more conventional Elizabethan woman than she may seem.

Portia's finest quality is her wit (meaning intellect). She can argue better than any other character in the play, and it is difficult to imagine anyone getting the better of her. This is shown most clearly in the trial scene. Portia outwits Shylock and makes him talk himself out of having his bond by getting him to insist that it is followed to the letter. Her appeal for mercy is moving and extremely effective. After this speech the audience is very definitely on the side of the Christians and Shylock appears to be a wicked man. Once she has won Antonio his freedom, we see the other side of her nature in two ways:

- Portia insists upon Shylock's goods and lands being seized. She wants him to beg for his life to the Duke and delights in humiliating him.

- Portia then behaves cruelly to Bassanio, her husband. She knows that it will be very hard for him to give up the ring she has given him, yet she insists upon it. She carries this on far past the point of a simple joke in some commentators' views.

In Act V, Portia takes great delight in making her husband feel uncomfortable. Again, it might be said that she goes too far with this. She behaves like Shylock; she has tricked Bassanio into swearing to a bond that she knows he cannot keep and then torments him for breaking it. Portia seems very much in control of the marriage, despite her earlier statement that Bassanio was her lord.

It is also quite possible that Portia knew that Antonio's ships had not sunk, well before she went to the trial. Towards the end of Act V, she gives Antonio a letter containing the good news, yet she has herself only just returned. If she did have the letter before the trial, then it need not have taken place and was all for Portia's amusement.

SHYLOCK

The way in which Shylock is portrayed on stage has changed considerably since the play was first performed, when he was made out to be a villain and a clown. This changed in the nineteenth century when the actor Edmund Kean played Shylock as an intelligent man who had been victimised. Certainly Shakespeare did not write Shylock as a simple, one-dimensional part. He is one of the most complex characters in English literature.

To a modern audience, Shylock is sometimes a victim and sometimes a villain. The Elizabethans would have held the much simpler view that the Christians were always right and so Shylock was always in the wrong.

We first see him in Act I Scene 3, when Bassanio and Antonio ask him for the loan of 3,000 ducats. Shylock is clearly plotting his revenge on Antonio, but our sympathy soon lies with the moneylender because of Antonio's bullying way with him.

Throughout Acts II and III, other characters add to this view that Shylock is victimised. Salerio and Solanio behave like Antonio, Launcelot leaves his service and even his own daughter deserts him. Apart from two brief episodes with Tubal, we never see Shylock with his own people, so we are usually given the Christians view of him. The Christians invite him to dinner on the night that Jessica elopes with Lorenzo, and so betray his trust further. Against all this is the fact that Shylock pursues his revenge upon Antonio. The lines 'I'll plague him, I'll torture him – I am glad of it' (III.1.110–11) show how bitter Shylock has become, yet we cannot help but feel that this is not all his fault. After years of being kicked and spat upon by men like Antonio, Shylock's hatred is understandable.

In the trial scene, he has the chance to show that he is far superior to the Christians. If Shylock were to show mercy to Antonio, then he would come out of the proceedings very well indeed. He does not show mercy, but presses on ruthlessly with his attempt to kill Antonio. When he is defeated by Portia, the audience is no longer on his side. If the play finished here, we would leave the theatre feeling that Shylock had probably got what he deserved. As it is, the harsh punishments he receives, first from Portia and then from Antonio, tend to shift sympathy back to Shylock. Perhaps the oddest thing about the end of the play is that Shylock does not feature in it at all. In the final part of the courtroom scene Shylock hardly speaks.

- **Highly intelligent**
- **True to his faith**
- **Victim of racism**
- **Bitter**
- **Driven by hatred**

 **EXAMINER'S SECRET**

You need to look at the extent to which Shylock deserves his fate. He is certainly unkind to his own daughter though he may have been driven to this.

BASSANIO

Bassanio is a headstrong young man. At the start of the play he says that he has wasted all his own fortune and a sum of money loaned to him by Antonio. He is a little too ready to fall in love with Portia and, at one stage, seems more interested in her money than in her. He is quite a shrewd character as he sees the danger of Antonio signing the bond. He is, however, still prepared to let his friend go ahead and make the promise to Shylock.

In the presence of Portia he changes his behaviour. His is no match for her wit and he becomes a little too keen too quickly. This nervousness shows his lack of experience with women. His long speeches before choosing the casket are comic as they are far too intense. He talks too much when excited and forgets to control his emotions in public.

True and loyal friend

Playboy

Honest

? DID YOU KNOW?

Bassanio is part of the happy ending of the play. You should consider whether he deserves to be so lucky.

He does prove to be a loyal friend to Antonio as he leaves his wife on their wedding day to travel to Venice and help him. He offers to exchange his life for Antonio's, at one point in the trial scene. Bassanio is rather naive as he thinks that he can simply talk Shylock out of taking the pound of flesh. He does not seem to realise the strength of the moneylender's feelings and so misjudges the situation. He has trouble keeping his temper, calling Shylock a 'cruel devil' (IV.1.213) yet expecting to win him over.

Bassanio shows that he is an honest man during the business with the rings. It really troubles him that he has to give his ring to the lawyer and yet he does it as he feels it is the right thing to do. When Portia presses him for an explanation as to why he is not wearing the ring, Bassanio tells the truth. He could have made up a story or have simply said that he had lost it; instead he owns up to having given it away to the first person who asked for it. Again he is not very good at hiding his feelings. He is a much simpler person than Portia and her comments about Bassanio being her 'lord' (III.2.165) seem out of place when we see the two together.

GRATIANO

Gratiano is looked upon by his friends as being a clown. He talks far too much and not always at the appropriate time. Bassanio has been in trouble before now because of Gratiano's behaviour and is sometimes embarrassed by him. Gratiano cannot resist the temptation to make a joke whenever possible and loves the sound of his own voice. Gratiano thinks that he, himself, is very funny.

He falls in love with Nerissa in the time it takes Bassanio to choose the casket. This rash behaviour is typical of him. He also makes a promise about the ring without thinking of the consequences.

During the courtroom scene he does not help the situation with his strong attacks upon Shylock. Many of the characters present at the trial think the same as Gratiano, but he is the one who comes out and says that Shylock is an 'inexorable dog' (IV.1.128). He is easily outwitted by Nerissa and becomes very frustrated with her when she does not believe his explanation.

NERISSA

Nerissa is Portia's maid, companion, and **confidante**. She seems to have modelled herself on Portia and generally follows what her mistress does. She can be quite crude, though she is never as sharp as Portia when making jokes. She is prepared to put Portia in her place when she starts to complain about the life she leads and so has some independence.

LAUNCELOT

Launcelot is a comic character who represents the ordinary citizens of Venice. He is not interested in the important dealings of Antonio and Bassanio unless they affect him. He is preoccupied with getting himself a good position in life and happily trades one master off against another. He does reveal that he is also subject to the same feelings as the Christians. He makes several unkind remarks about Shylock. Launcelot is devoted to Jessica and has formed a genuine friendship with her, though he is not very sensitive in the comments he makes about her father.

He serves to lighten the atmosphere of the play and his appearances tend to follow very dramatic moments. He also gives the other characters, such as Lorenzo, someone to make fun of.

Clownish
Funny

SALERIO AND SOLANIO

The two men are quite wealthy citizens, though they are clearly looking for an opportunity to better themselves. They see Antonio as a good contact and are rather jealous of the attention that he shows to Bassanio. They act as narrators, filling in information on events that would have taken too long to portray on stage. They also reinforce the strongly anti-Semitic atmosphere of Venice; their comments about Shylock are as unpleasant as anyone's.

THE DUKE

As ruler of the State of Venice, he is the most powerful and wealthy man in the city and has the final say in major disputes. He appears to be fair, as he does not want to see Antonio killed, but equally, he does not break the laws of Venice simply to defeat Shylock. This might make him a poor ruler as he is not prepared to sacrifice his own reputation in order to see that justice prevails.

JESSICA

Torn between romantic and family love

The daughter of Shylock and so Jewish herself, she renounces her beliefs and disowns her father in order to be with the man she loves. She is quite cruel in the way that she leaves and unfair when she steals from Shylock. In fact the way she behaves towards Shylock makes a modern audience feel sympathetic towards him. Like the other lovers, she has made a decision quickly and the suggestion is that she might live to regret this. In the scenes at Belmont, Jessica is largely ignored by the other characters, especially Portia. Her conversation with Lorenzo at the beginning of Act V features stories of lovers who have betrayed one another and this points to possible difficulties ahead for this couple. Even though Jessica converts to Christianity, she may well not be properly accepted by the likes of Portia and Antonio.

LORENZO

A Christian and an associate of Bassanio, he has fallen in love with Jessica, though it is unlikely that the two of them could have met frequently as they come from different cultures. He takes her away from Venice without really having anywhere to take her to. They roam Italy spending huge sums of money unwisely and then arrive in Belmont and stay in the house of someone neither of them know. This shows that Lorenzo has not planned his future with Jessica and has failed to consider how a Christian with a Jewish wife will be received. Perhaps the conversation about doomed lovers is more relevant than he thinks.

GOBBO

Old Gobbo, father of Launcelot, is nearly blind and easily confused. He fails at first to recognise his own son, but tries to help Launcelot to obtain a position with Bassanio. He often chooses the wrong word for the occasion, with comic effect.

THE PRINCES OF MOROCCO AND ARRAGON

A proud man who feels that he has as much right to marry Portia as anyone, Morocco is pompous and full of himself but proves to be honourable. Morocco can be played as a fool or as an important man who suffers discrimination at the hands of Portia.

Arragon is long-winded and full of his own importance. It should be remembered that Ar(r)agon was a Spanish kingdom and that the English and the Spanish had been bitter enemies for many years. The Prince of Arragon is an Englishman's idea of a Spaniard.

LANGUAGE AND STYLE

Students make common errors when starting to talk about the writer's use of language. It is probably one of the more difficult aspects of literature. In this section you will be given some information about the language used by Shakespeare and some pointers as to how to go about discussing it.

The first, and most obvious, thing about the language used in *The Merchant of Venice* is that it is all speech. This may seem an obvious thing to say about a play but there are rules about the type of speech used at certain times and by certain characters.

There are two different types of speech used in the play: blank verse and prose.

EXAMINER'S SECRET
A candidate who is capable of arriving at unusual, well-supported judgements *independently* is likely to receive the highest marks.

BLANK VERSE

Most of the characters speak in blank verse. This is different from the way we normally speak. Verse has a rhythm, meaning that all the lines follow the same pattern.

Here is a line of verse from the play: 'You know me well, and herein spend but time' (I.1.153).

The line has ten beats to it, in its arrangement of stressed and unstressed syllables. The line which follows it also has ten beats to it: 'To wind about my love with circumstance' (I.1.154).

These are examples of blank verse. It is called 'blank' because it does not rhyme. This type of speech is used in two situations:

- Formal speech between important characters

- When something important is being said

Blank verse might seem rather an unusual convention to us but consider some conventions that we take for granted:

- Television advertisements are around thirty seconds long.

- Music chart singles are rarely over three minutes long.

- No matter what happens to Superman he will always come out on top!

We accept these conventions because we have grown used to them or indeed never known anything else. Shakespeare's audience would have been comfortable with the stage conventions of the day.

Occasionally, a character speaks in rhyme. This is to let the audience know either that something important is being said or that a scene is about to end. Remember, there were not the breaks in performance due to lighting changes that we have in the theatre today. Plays were performed in the open air and in daylight. Rhyme was one device that could assist the audience in recognising an important element of the play.

? DID YOU KNOW?

Verse is a convention that would have been recognised by the audience.

PROSE

When we speak in everyday situations we do not speak in blank verse. Imagine how difficult it would be if everything we said had to be fitted into a pattern like the one above. What we would think of as *normal speech* is called prose. There are clear situations in which prose is used:

- When characters are relaxed and talking about unimportant matters

- By unimportant characters

- By uneducated characters in order to make them seem rather rough

The way in which a character uses language helps the audience to decide what sort of person he/she is. Here are some examples of different uses of language:

- When Antonio is depressed he speaks very formally and seems unable to relax.

- Shylock repeats the same phrase, 'I would have my bond' (IV.1.87). This shows he is preoccupied with the idea of revenge.

- Bassanio is excited when speaking about Portia and uses strong classical imagery to describe her; 'And she is fair, and fairer than that word, Of wondrous virtues' (I.1.162 3), and 'many Jasons come in quest of her' (I.1.172). Here, Bassanio's speech gives the audience clues about his character. He seems rash, foolishly romantic and very interested in money. It is not one of the other characters who lets us know this but Bassanio himself.

- All the lovers get carried away when describing their partners.

  They use the language of love poetry, showing the intensity of their feelings. There was a convention in Shakespeare's day known as **courtly love**. The language of courtly love was well understood. Lovers were expected to describe one another's finest attributes. A man would describe a woman's beauty in terms of her skin, eyes, hair and voice: a woman might talk about a man's strength, figure or charm.

DID YOU KNOW?
Verse is much easier to learn than **prose**.

DID YOU KNOW?
The Elizabethans were quite familiar with the language of **courtly love**.

EXAMINER'S SECRET

Keep a quotation book – select the key quotations and put them into a little book – this way you will get to know them far more easily than searching for them every time in a 125-page play.

Look at the way the lovers talk in Act III Scene 2.

> **Fair Portia's counterfeit! What demi-god**
> **Hath come so near creation?**   (III.2.115–16)

Such speech shows the depth of feeling and the level of excitement of the characters.

Sometimes, however, they try too hard.

- Launcelot tries to use clever words, but fails. This shows that he would like to climb up the social ladder but is unlikely to be able to.

The use of comic characters is very important as it allows the playwright to control tension. The audience cannot be in a state of nervous tension for three hours. Introducing comic characters at key points in a drama can relax the tension and allow it to be built up again to a higher level.

When you are taking about language try to understand why the writer has used particular words and phrases. Is Hamlet's famous line, 'To be or not to be, that is the question' (III.1.56) more effective than 'Should I kill myself?' Most people would say 'yes' but you have to look at why.

Style is all in the way that the thing is said. Some writers are simply better at this than others.

Remember the following points about any text you read:

- The writer started off with a blank page.

- Every word has been written – it is not real. (You could say that the text is a **construct**.)

- One form of words may be far more effective than another in getting across a particular idea or feeling.

- The writer set out to do something – not simply to fill the page – you have to identify what this aim was.

- You should discuss whether the writer has been effective e.g. is a frightening passage actually frightening?

Finally, try to develop an appreciation for style. This can only be done by reading the work of different writers. You need to have your own opinion as to how good Shakespeare is at expressing ideas and emotions.

 **EXAMINER'S SECRET**

As you write, check that you are still answering the question. It is surprisingly easy to start well and drift off the subject entirely.

Now take a break!

PART FOUR

RESOURCES

How to Use Quotations

One of the secrets of success in writing essays is the way you use quotations. There are five basic principles:

1 Put inverted commas at the beginning and end of the quotation.

2 Write the quotation exactly as it appears in the original.

3 Do not use a quotation that repeats what you have just written.

4 Use the quotation so that it fits into your sentence.

5 Keep the quotation as short as possible.

Quotations should be used to develop the line of thought in your essays. Your comment should not duplicate what is in your quotation. For example:

> **Shylock warns us that he is as fierce as a dog: 'since I am a dog, beware my fangs'.** (III.3.7)

Far more effective is to write:

> **Shylock's revenge springs from his inhuman treatment by Christians: 'since I am a dog, beware my fangs'.** (III.3.7)

Always lay out the lines as they appear in the text. For example:

> **Bassanio encourages Gratiano to have some fun at the party,**
>   **'... for we have friends**
>   **That purpose merriment'.** (II.3.199–200)

or

> **Bassanio encourages Gratiano to have some fun at the party,**
> **'... for we have friends / That purpose merriment'.** (II.3.199–200)

EXAMINER'S SECRET
Short, snappy quotations are always the best.

EXAMINER'S SECRET
In a typical examination you might use as many as eight quotations.

However, the most sophisticated way of using the writer's words is to embed them into your sentence:

> **Shylock warns those who have treated him as 'a dog' to 'beware my fangs'.**   (III.3.7)

When you use quotations in this way, you are demonstrating the ability to use text as evidence to support your ideas – not simply including words from the original to prove you have read it.

COURSEWORK ESSAY

Set aside an hour or so at the start of your work to plan what you have to do.

- List all the points you feel are needed to cover the task. Collect page references of information and quotations that will support what you have to say. A helpful tool is the highlighter pen: this saves painstaking copying and enables you to target precisely what you want to use.

- Focus on what you consider to be the main points of the essay. Try to sum up your argument in a single sentence, which could be the closing sentence of your essay. Depending on the essay title, it could be a statement about a character: Portia is the wittiest character in the play. She is very good at playing word games with Bassanio and Nerissa and it is Portia who outwits Shylock when all other attempts have failed; an opinion about a setting: I believe that Shylock is a product of the environment in which he has lived. He has been made cruel by years of ill treatment; or a judgement on a theme: I think the main theme of the play is that life is full of trials. Some are trials of loyalty, others are tests to see whether someone can tell right from wrong.

- Make a short essay plan. Use the first paragraph to introduce the argument you wish to make. In the following paragraphs develop this argument with details, examples and other possible points of view. Sum up your argument in the last paragraph. Check you have answered the question.

EXAMINER'S SECRET
It is always a good idea to collect a range of words to describe a character.

- Write the essay, remembering all the time the central point you are making.

- On completion, go back over what you have written to eliminate careless errors and improve expression. Read it aloud to yourself, or, if you are feeling more confident, to a relative or friend.

If you can, try to type your essay using a word processor. This will allow you to correct and improve your writing without spoiling its appearance.

EXAMINER'S SECRET

Always read the whole examination paper before you start writing.

SITTING THE EXAMINATION

Examination papers are carefully designed to give you the opportunity to do your best. Follow these handy hints for exam success:

BEFORE YOU START

- Make sure you know the subject of the examination so that you are properly prepared and equipped.

- You need to be comfortable and free from distractions. Inform the invigilator if anything is off-putting, e.g. a shaky desk.

- Read the instructions, or rubric, on the front of the examination paper. You should know by now what you have to do but check to reassure yourself.

- Observe the time allocation – and follow it carefully. If they recommend 60 minutes for Question 1 and 30 minutes for Question 2, it is because Question 1 carries twice as many marks.

- Consider the mark allocation. You should write a longer response for 4 marks than for 2 marks.

WRITING YOUR RESPONSES

- Use the questions to structure your response, e.g. question: 'The endings of X's poems are always particularly significant. Explain their importance with reference to two poems.' The first part of your answer will describe the ending of the first poem; the second part will look at the ending of the second poem; the third part will be an explanation of the significance of the two endings.

- Write a brief draft outline of your response.

- A typical 30-minute examination essay is probably between 400 and 600 words in length.

- Keep your writing legible and easy to read, using paragraphs to show the structure of your answers.

- Spend a couple of minutes afterwards quickly checking for obvious errors.

WHEN YOU HAVE FINISHED

- Don't be downhearted – if you found the examination difficult, it is probably because you really worked at the questions. Let's face it, they are not meant to be easy!

- Don't pay too much attention to what your friends have to say about the paper. Everyone's experience is different and no two people ever give the same answers.

IMPROVE YOUR GRADE

Most students can immediately make some improvement in grade by recognising what it is that they are being asked to do. All written tasks can be broken down into the following simple areas:

- What did the writer set out to do?

- How did the writer go about doing it?

- Was the writer successful?

WHAT DID THE WRITER SET OUT TO DO?

You should consider the first point before you begin to write any lengthy answer. You must try to grasp what the writer had set out to do. In other words, was Shakespeare simply filling up three hours of

EXAMINER'S SECRET

An A-grade candidate can analyse a variety of the writer's techniques.

EXAMINER'S SECRET

Higher-level achievement begins at the point when you show you are aware of being marked.

stage time with *The Merchant of Venice*? The plot could be summarised in a few pages, so why does the play take three hours on stage?

You might want to consider areas such as social comment. It is possible that Shakespeare was interested in raising issues such as the treatment of foreign cultures in England. To have done so directly would have been dangerous, as the Church was immensely powerful in Elizabethan England. Any suggestion that the Jew, Shylock, or the Moor, Morocco, might have been honourable men could well have landed Shakespeare in serious trouble – England was a staunchly Protestant country under Elizabeth and was in political and religious turmoil for the early part of the reign of James I.

In spite of these difficulties, Shakespeare set about writing Shylock as a real character, not simply a Jew who was there to be poked fun at. You need to consider whether Shakespeare realised that Shylock could be portrayed in such a way as to appear sympathetic at times. (Shylock could certainly not have been portrayed sympathetically on the stage in Shakespeare's time.) It is one of the mysteries surrounding Shakespeare's work. How could he have known that he was creating characters that could be played in different ways according to the times?

There were many playwrights of Shakespeare's day whose work is no longer performed so perhaps Shakespeare was doing something a little different from his fellow writers. The plot of *The Merchant of Venice* is quite complicated but it is the way that Shakespeare handles the various elements of plot that makes the play interesting. Look at the way that one part of the plot is built up to the point where a major event is about to take place and then the scene shifts to another area of plot altogether. This control of tension – making the audience wait – is a major element of Shakespeare's craft.

Remember: Shakespeare was a professional wrier and he needed to please his audience.

How did the writer go about doing it?

Many students concentrate on the second point only: how did the writer write the piece? This results in a lengthy retelling of the story of whatever it is they have just read. There is nothing wrong with some account of the story but if this is all you do then you have carried out a fairly basic task. The plot of most great novels, plays and poems could be given to a class of eight-year-olds. They would then retell the story and draw a lovely picture. The skills shown by the eight-year-old students would not amount to much.

Remember: simply retelling the story is not a high level skill.

WAS THE WRITER SUCCESSFUL?

When you do come to discuss the way that the writer went about achieving his aims, there are some basic things that you need to do:

- Decide what it is you want to say
- Select the parts of the text that support what you want to say (see **How to use quotations**)

All too often students make sweeping statements without backing them up. Try to make your comments precise and to keep them in focus with regard to the question you are answering. A question on justice in *The Merchant of Venice* does not require a discussion of the comic scenes between Launcelot and Gobbo.

To reach the highest level you need to consider whether the writer has been successful. If you think Shakespeare set out to create believable female characters, has he managed this? Do you think Shakespeare intended us to feel some sympathy for Shylock and, if so, has he made us feel it?

This area of your answer should reflect what you identified at the start regarding what the writer set out to do. If a horror film is not frightening then it is not successful: think in this way about the play. You need to consider whether *The Merchant of Venice* works as a drama.

A higher-level answer will always contain the personal response of the student. Do not be afraid to say **'I feel that ...'** or **'I believe ...'**. You must of course have some evidence for what you suggest. There are people who still think the Earth is flat but there is pretty good evidence that it is not.

EXAMINER'S SECRET
You will not get high marks simply by retelling the story.

EXAMINER'S SECRET

Don't waste time looking at how your friends are doing!

Each time you make a major point you should support it, either by giving an account in your own words or by using a quotation.

Two major elements of language which tend to be seen by only the best students are **imagery** and wit.

● You need to show how the use of imagery is responsible for creating particular impressions. For example, in Act IV Scene 1 (lines 128–38) Gratiano uses several words for dog and ends up comparing Shylock to a wolf. Dogs and wolves are associated with certain types of behaviour. Gratiano is not saying that Shylock actually is a wolf but that he shows no mercy to his victims and strikes when they are at their weakest. This is how a wolf behaves. Consider the effect of substituting the dove for the wolf. The whole tone of speech would change. This is because we have set ideas about the dove which are very different to those we hold about the wolf.

● Writers know these associations and play upon them for effect. Take the simplest idea of all – villain dressed in black; good guy dressed in white. Such basic images occur throughout the history of world literature. Good writers do not simply use such basic images. They are constantly looking out for new things to use as comparisons. You need to recognise that this is how writers work and include references to it in your written answers.

● Wit is a very big part of conversation in Shakespeare's plays. We would call wit 'intelligence'. Portia and Bassanio try to outwit one another. Launcelot tries it with Jessica with comic results.

The final point to bear in mind is that your own writing needs to be of a high standard. You must attempt to use the language of literary criticism when discussing a work of literature. Simply saying '**the play was good**' does not really mean anything. It does not matter whether you liked the play; the important thing to remember is that you are commenting on the effectiveness of the work. Using vocabulary beyond that you might normally use when talking to your friends is vital if you wish to come across well on paper.

ANSWERING QUESTIONS

If we consider three levels of answer that can be called basic, better and best, you might find it useful to see the key features of these answers from the examiner's viewpoint.

Basic

Students tend to re-tell the story no matter what the question is. Many simple comments will be made without support, e.g. **'Shylock is not very nice to Antonio'**.

An answer at the basic level is usually a series of such simple statements and contains no real understanding of the thoughts of the writer, in fact the writer is rarely considered at all.

Better

At this level students will pay some attention to the question that has been asked and make some connected comments with support from the text.

Statements will be more detailed and will largely be supported with direct references taken from the text. This can lead to a rather mechanical form of writing with a string of comments and quotations one after the other. There will often be long passages of narrative that are repeated for no particular reason.

Best

The best candidates feel no need to tell the story. They realise that the examiner knows the play. Such candidates are able to concentrate on the specific demands of the question and are comfortable with the idea that the play has been written with a purpose and audience in mind.

Quotations will often be integrated into the student's own writing rather than tacked on afterwards. Above all there will be a sense of the effects achieved by the writer.

EXAMINER'S SECRET

If you are asked to make a comparison, use comparing words such as, 'on the other hand', 'however' and 'by contrast'.

Don't forget the things you need to cover:

- What did the writer set out to do?

- How did the writer go about doing it?

- Was the writer successful?

Good luck wiith your writing about Shakespeare.

SAMPLE ESSAY PLAN

EXAMINER'S SECRET
You are always given credit for writing your essay plans.

A typical essay question on *The Merchant of Venice* is followed by a sample essay plan in note form. This does not present the only answer to the question, merely one. Do not be afraid to include your own ideas, and leave out some of those in the sample!

How much do you think Shylock has been influenced by the environment in which he lives?

The essay needs an introduction, main argument and a conclusion.

INTRODUCTION
Shylock is useful to the Christians only because he does something which they are not allowed to do.

PART 1
Explain what his particular environment is; the points below develop this idea:

- In Act I Scene 3, Bassanio is effectively going to his local bank to ask for a loan, yet he is not always polite.

- Antonio kicks and spits at Shylock simply because he does not like the way the moneylender does business – quote examples of Antonio's behaviour.

- In Act II Scene 2, Launcelot, Shylock's servant, gives a disrespectful opinion of his master. His words are full of anti-Semitic remarks and some of his jokes are in poor taste.

- In Act III Scene 1, Salerio and Solanio continue the victimisation of Shylock, even though they know he is upset at his daughter's disappearance.

This establishes the type of behaviour that Shylock had to put up with. Mention the law always being on the side of the Christians, and Jews having to wear special clothes to make them stand out.

EXAMINER'S SECRET
Always have a spare pen!

PART 2

The next stage is to look at the type of man he is:

- When going about his own business

- When confronted by the Christians

The two scenes with Tubal show Shylock with a fellow Jew. Look at how Tubal regards Shylock, e.g. in Act III Scene 1, Tubal is not particularly sympathetic towards Shylock. Tubal probably suffers the same treatment as Shylock yet he seems less bitter. Here are some other situations to consider:

- Shylock does not have a very close relationship with Jessica.

- He wants to see his daughter punished rather than wanting to forgive her.

- When confronted by the Christians, Shylock fights his corner:

- He tricks Antonio into swearing to the bond.

- He is delighted to hear that Antonio's ships have been lost.

- He takes great delight in taunting Gratiano, Bassanio and Antonio.

- He goes too far in his search for revenge.

- He is foolish enough to try to use the Christian laws against a Christian.

- He is severely punished for his attempt on Antonio's life.

Shylock's big mistake is to think that the law can be used for his benefit.

EXAMINER'S SECRET

Everything you write on your answer sheet is marked.

CONCLUSION

No definite answer

- Shylock has been more strongly affected by his treatment than other Jews have.

- He is partly the product of his environment but some of his behaviour is because of his own character.

- His character has been formed whilst living in this society and so the harsh treatment he receives is responsible for a large degree of his hatred.

FURTHER QUESTIONS

Make a plan as shown above and attempt these questions.

1. By examining his treatment of Portia and Shylock, discuss the idea that Shakespeare was neither racist nor sexist.

2. People tend to be shaped by the environment in which they live. By exploring the behaviour of any two characters from *The Merchant of Venice*, say how true you think this is.

3. The play is full of trials. Say what any two of the following reveal about the characters involved:
   - The test of the caskets
   - Shylock and Antonio in court
   - The test of the rings

4. The play deals with different ideas of right and wrong. Examine the feelings and actions of two of the following characters and say what each one feels about this idea:
   - Shylock
   - Portia
   - Antonio
   - Jessica

5 Discuss the way in which Shakespeare explores the different kinds of bonds which exist between people. You should consider:
- The bond of friendship
- The bond of marriage
- Bonds made in business

6 'Belmont is a woman's world, whilst Venice is a man's' – consider this quotation.

7 What do you learn about the Elizabethan view of the world from the attitudes shown in the play?

8 Discuss the difficulties and advantages of staging the play today.

9 Say what you learn from the play about the idea of justice in Elizabethan England.

10 Act V is quite different from the rest of the play. Say how far you think Act V is a successful conclusion to the events of *The Merchant of Venice*.

EXAMINER'S SECRET

Examiners **never** take marks away.

Now take a break!

blank verse lines which have rhythm, but do not rhyme. Most of the play is in blank verse, with **iambic pentameter** as the type of verse used

confidant(e) a friend of the chief character whom he/she entrusts with information, providing a useful method of letting the audience know his/her motives

courtly love a convention in Elizabethan England. Lovers tended to talk in a certain way and to obey clear rules regarding courtship

construct an invention of the writer, crafted for a purpose

iambic pentameter a line of poetry with five pairs of syllables arranged in the following order: unstressed then stressed. Most of the speeches in the play are in iambic pentameter e.g. 'But còme, I'll tèll thee àll my whòle de–vìce' (III.4.81)

imagery an image is a picture in words. There are two obvious kinds of imagery – **simile** and **metaphor**. Imagery is used extensively by writers, indeed it is difficult to say very much without using imagery

malapropism using the wrong word without realising it. The word 'malapropism' comes from the character Mrs Malaprop in Sheridan's play *The Rivals* (1775). She continually tried to impress by using long words, but ended up speaking nonsense. This was known in Shakespeare's day as 'cacozelia'

metaphor a description of one thing in terms of something else: for example, Morocco says 'A golden mind stoops not to shows of dross' (II.7.20). Morocco is speaking metaphorically – no one has a mind that is actually made of gold

prose what we would call 'ordinary speech', prose has no set pattern of rhythm

pun a play on words. The Elizabethans were very fond of puns and they considered that someone who could pun well was intelligent. Sometimes this can go too far, as Lorenzo points out to Launcelot, and is used for comic effect when a character puns at every opportunity

rhyming couplet adjacent lines of any verse form which rhyme

simile A direct comparison of one thing to another: for example, Antonio says 'An evil soul producing holy witness / Is like a villain with a smiling cheek' (I.3.95–6)

CHECKPOINT 1 Shakespeare is introducing the idea of Antonio's losses.

CHECKPOINT 2 So that Portia can reveal her true feelings to the audience.

CHECKPOINT 3 This is because formal business is about to be conducted.

CHECKPOINT 4 In Shakespeare's day it was normal to laugh at black people. Today a director might well choose to make Morocco a sympathetic character.

CHECKPOINT 5 That Gobbo is not as clever as he thinks. He copies the speech of educated men without really realising what he is saying.

CHECKPOINT 6 He does not seem to be the most attentive father.

CHECKPOINT 7 Bassanio is happy to waste Antonio's money.

CHECKPOINT 8 In order to keep the audience waiting and develop the dramatic tension of the scene.

CHECKPOINT 9 Clearly we are meant to think that this might be one of Antonio's ships.

CHECKPOINT 10 There may be an element of joy in Tubal's feelings here.

CHECKPOINT 11 Portia likes to think of herself as strong but she also feels sorry for herself.

CHECKPOINT 12 Portia might well know what is in the caskets. She certainly knows gold and silver do not contain her portrait. She would be very nervous as Bassanio discussed the wrong caskets first.

CHECKPOINT 13 Perhaps Portia is more of an Elizabethan woman than she might like to think.

CHECKPOINT 14 Portia is clever and scheming.

CHECKPOINT 15 She is tricking him into insisting on the exact wording of the bond.

CHECKPOINT 16 Antonio certainly shows none of the Christian mercy that he expected from Shylock.

CHECKPOINT 17 The plot moves from being very serious to quite light-hearted.

CHECKPOINT 18 They highlight the typical behaviour of lovers – in contrast to the actions of Portia.

CHECKPOINT 19 Portia is clearly setting up the business about the missing rings.

CHECKPOINT 20 In order to create tension by moving between locations.

Test yourself (Act i)

1 Antonio (*Scene 1*)

2 Bassanio (*Scene 1*)

3 Antonio (*Scene 3*)

4 Portia (*Scene 2*)

5 Shylock (*Scene 3*)

6 Antonio (*Scene 3*)

7 Shylock (*Scene 3*)

8 Bassanio (*Scene 1*)

9 Antonio (*Scene 1*)

Test yourself (Act ii)

1 Portia (*Scene 1*)

2 Launcelot (*Scene 2*)

3 Jessica (*Scene 3*)

4 Shylock (*Scene 5*)

5 Solanio reporting Shylock's words (*Scene 8*)

6 Lorenzo (*Scene 6*)

7 Morocco (*Scene 7*)

8 Portia (*Scene 9*)

Test yourself (Act iii)

1 Portia (*Scene 2*)

2 Bassanio (*Scene 2*)

3 Jessica (*Scene 2*)

4 Antonio (*Scene 3*)

5 Launcelot (*Scene 5*)

6 Lorenzo (*Scene 5*)

7 Antonio (*Scene 2*)

8 Antonio (*Scene 3*)

9 Shylock (*Scene 2*)

Test yourself (Act iv)

1 The duke (*Scene 1*)

2 Shylock (*Scene 1*)

3 Bassanio (*Scene 1*)

4 Gratiano (*Scene 1*)

5 Portia (*Scene 1*)

6 Shylock (*Scene 1*)

7 Portia (*Scene 1*)

8 To Shylock, about Portia (*Scene 1*)

9 Shylock (*Scene 1*)

Test yourself (Act v)

1 Lorenzo (*Scene 1*)

2 Jessica (*Scene 1*)

3 Launcelot (*Scene 1*)

4 Portia (*Scene 1*)

5 Portia (*Scene 1*)

6 Gratiano (*Scene 1*)

7 Portia (*Scene 1*)

8 Launcelot (*Scene 1*)

9 Bassanio (*Scene 1*)

10 Portia (*Scene 1*)

NOTES

Maya Angelou
I Know Why the Caged Bird Sings

Jane Austen
Pride and Prejudice

Alan Ayckbourn
Absent Friends

Elizabeth Barrett Browning
Selected Poems

Robert Bolt
A Man for All Seasons

Harold Brighouse
Hobson's Choice

Charlotte Brontë
Jane Eyre

Emily Brontë
Wuthering Heights

Shelagh Delaney
A Taste of Honey

Charles Dickens
David Copperfield
Great Expectations
Hard Times
Oliver Twist

Roddy Doyle
Paddy Clarke Ha Ha Ha

George Eliot
Silas Marner
The Mill on the Floss

Anne Frank
The Diary of a Young Girl

William Golding
Lord of the Flies

Oliver Goldsmith
She Stoops to Conquer

Willis Hall
The Long and the Short and the Tall

Thomas Hardy
Far from the Madding Crowd

The Mayor of Casterbridge
Tess of the d'Urbervilles
The Withered Arm and other Wessex Tales

L.P. Hartley
The Go-Between

Seamus Heaney
Selected Poems

Susan Hill
I'm the King of the Castle

Barry Hines
A Kestrel for a Knave

Louise Lawrence
Children of the Dust

Harper Lee
To Kill a Mockingbird

Laurie Lee
Cider with Rosie

Arthur Miller
The Crucible
A View from the Bridge

Robert O'Brien
Z for Zachariah

Frank O'Connor
My Oedipus Complex and Other Stories

George Orwell
Animal Farm

J.B. Priestley
An Inspector Calls
When We Are Married

Willy Russell
Educating Rita
Our Day Out

J.D. Salinger
The Catcher in the Rye

William Shakespeare
Henry IV Part I
Henry V
Julius Caesar

Macbeth
The Merchant of Venice
A Midsummer Night's Dream
Much Ado About Nothing
Romeo and Juliet
The Tempest
Twelfth Night

George Bernard Shaw
Pygmalion

Mary Shelley
Frankenstein

R.C. Sherriff
Journey's End

Rukshana Smith
Salt on the snow

John Steinbeck
Of Mice and Men

Robert Louis Stevenson
Dr Jekyll and Mr Hyde

Jonathan Swift
Gulliver's Travels

Robert Swindells
Daz 4 Zoe

Mildred D. Taylor
Roll of Thunder, Hear My Cry

Mark Twain
Huckleberry Finn

James Watson
Talking in Whispers

Edith Wharton
Ethan Frome

William Wordsworth
Selected Poems

A Choice of Poets

Mystery Stories of the Nineteenth Century including The Signalman

Nineteenth Century Short Stories

Poetry of the First World War

Six Women Poets

Margaret Atwood
Cat's Eye
The Handmaid's Tale

Jane Austen
Emma
Mansfield Park
Persuasion
Pride and Prejudice
Sense and Sensibility

Alan Bennett
Talking Heads

William Blake
Songs of Innocence and of Experience

Charlotte Brontë
Jane Eyre
Villette

Emily Brontë
Wuthering Heights

Angela Carter
Nights at the Circus

Geoffrey Chaucer
The Franklin's Prologue and Tale
The Miller's Prologue and Tale
The Prologue to the Canterbury Tales
The Wife of Bath's Prologue and Tale

Samuel Coleridge
Selected Poems

Joseph Conrad
Heart of Darkness

Daniel Defoe
Moll Flanders

Charles Dickens
Bleak House
Great Expectations
Hard Times

Emily Dickinson
Selected Poems

John Donne
Selected Poems

Carol Ann Duffy
Selected Poems

George Eliot
Middlemarch
The Mill on the Floss

T.S. Eliot
Selected Poems
The Waste Land

F. Scott Fitzgerald
The Great Gatsby

E.M. Forster
A Passage to India

Brian Friel
Translations

Thomas Hardy
Jude the Obscure
The Mayor of Casterbridge
The Return of the Native
Selected Poems
Tess of the d'Urbervilles

Seamus Heaney
Selected Poems from 'Opened Ground'

Nathaniel Hawthorne
The Scarlet Letter

Homer
The Iliad
The Odyssey

Aldous Huxley
Brave New World

Kazuo Ishiguro
The Remains of the Day

Ben Jonson
The Alchemist

James Joyce
Dubliners

John Keats
Selected Poems

Christopher Marlowe
Doctor Faustus
Edward II

Arthur Miller
Death of a Salesman

John Milton
Paradise Lost Books I & II

Toni Morrison
Beloved

George Orwell
Nineteen Eighty-Four

Sylvia Plath
Selected Poems

Alexander Pope
Rape of the Lock & Selected Poems

William Shakespeare
Antony and Cleopatra
As You Like It
Hamlet
Henry IV Part I
King Lear
Macbeth
Measure for Measure
The Merchant of Venice
A Midsummer Night's Dream
Much Ado About Nothing
Othello
Richard II
Richard III
Romeo and Juliet
The Taming of the Shrew
The Tempest
Twelfth Night
The Winter's Tale

George Bernard Shaw
Saint Joan

Mary Shelley
Frankenstein

Jonathan Swift
Gulliver's Travels and A Modest Proposal

Alfred Tennyson
Selected Poems

Virgil
The Aeneid

Alice Walker
The Color Purple

Oscar Wilde
The Importance of Being Earnest

Tennessee Williams
A Streetcar Named Desire

Jeanette Winterson
Oranges Are Not the Only Fruit

John Webster
The Duchess of Malfi

Virginia Woolf
To the Lighthouse

W.B. Yeats
Selected Poems

Metaphysical Poets